Wh

A Personal Journal of Recovery... and Hope

John L.

© 2015 John L.
All rights reserved.
ISBN: 1514892677
ISBN 13: 9781514892671

DEDICATION

To all of the people who've helped me
over the years by telling me the truth,
whether I wanted to hear it or not;
you saved me...

Sobriety and my relationship with God
have always been my first priority—they go
hand in hand, and I can't have one without the other.
This book is especially dedicated to my second priority, Kandy
(who's been okay with that from the start).
Without her prompting, this story
might never have been told.

INTRODUCTION

My name is John L., and I'm a real alcoholic. What follows is my story, starting years before I finally got sober, and what's happened since. It is an account without any whitewashing of events—only *my* experience.

Just as in anyone's life, there are things I've done that I'm not proud of and found to be embarrassing as I wrote this. There are also highpoints in my life that I cannot, in good conscience, take credit for.

As I describe my journey of recovery, it is my hope that it may serve its intended purpose: to show that anyone, with enough willingness, in spite of life's adversities—self-inflicted or not—can accomplish anything…

Chapter 1
Blinded by the Glare

Perceptions are often likened to looking through the facets of a highly polished precious stone. Everyone has his or her own priceless "life stone," not only requiring periodic examination but possibly chiseling and polishing from time to time. Each surface of a "life stone" illuminates either unique qualities or imperfections, depending on what angle a person is looking at it from. In some cases, an individual can be so blinded by the brilliance of his or her stone's facets (because of an overinflated ego and pride) that what is all too obvious as a glaring flaw to others is often indiscernible to the sightless one. This can manifest itself in a kind of delusional thinking that I suffered from for years without knowing it.

Invariably, all human beings so blinded by one aspect of their "life stone" have reflected on their life experiences and had thoughts similar to: *I'm a good guy (or woman) working hard to make my way in this world, and everyone is out to get me* (some people call this the conspiracy theory); *If I only had this or that, I would be happy; Nobody appreciates the things I do for them; Why doesn't he or she love me the way I need to be loved?; What's in it for me?;* or *Nobody understands me.* Alcoholics and addicts will take this line of thinking even further: *You wouldn't want to have anything to do with me if you <u>really</u> had a clue what a lowlife I am and the things I've done; I don't deserve the good things in life that I see coming to everyone else; I'm going to hurt people if they don't do what I want them to do.*

With these self-absorbed dialogues going on between my ears, perceptions and my reactions to them served as major barriers to seeing reality for what it was, without any distortions. Over the course of time, I eventually found myself backed into a corner with no way out...

The very first time I got loaded, I drank like an alcoholic right from the get-go. During the summer of 1971, before my sophomore year of high school, a friend's parents were out of town, so a bunch of us pooled our money together to buy booze and have a party. I ended up chugging an entire bottle of Cold Bear wine (I don't even know if the wine had any grapes in it at all) and immediately paid the price for it. I spent the rest of the night sitting on the bathroom floor with my arms wrapped around the "porcelain school bus" having the dry heaves. Out of the corner of my eye, I saw my friends whooping and hollering, running up and down the hallway and having a good time. I thought to myself *I didn't get this right,* so I tried for the next umpteen years to get it right but was always undershooting or overshooting the mark. Normal people don't have a reaction like that. If they did what I did and suffered those kinds of consequences, they wouldn't do it again.

    I lived in a really small town in northern Maine with a population of about two hundred. A few months later, I was sneaking across Main Street in the middle of the night with a grocery bag in each arm filled with bottles of booze. One of the bags broke, and a bottle hit the asphalt shattering on impact, and all I could do was stand there and cry. Normal people don't behave that way. I didn't get loaded every day but did every chance I could.

    During the summer of 1976, I met the love of my life while working as a manager trainee at a retail store, Pic-Way Shoes, on Cleveland's far east side. Kandy worked at the submarine sandwich shop next door, and everyday I'd find an excuse to go over and order a Diet Coke or something just so I could check her out. It took a couple of months to build up enough courage to finally ask her out. We went on a date and eventually moved in together for a few years when, after losing several jobs, my sole source of income was from being a small-time dope smuggler. I asked her to marry me several times and could never understand why she said no. My last dope deal in Cleveland backfired, and I decided that we needed to separate for awhile to ensure our safety. I quickly moved back to Maine, living with my parents, and she stayed with relatives in southern California. I earned enough money to put together a small nest egg in order for us to relocate together to the west coast during the next five or six months as we talked regularly on the phone.

    We met in Cleveland, and I think it's ironic in a way that we crossed the border into California on April Fools' Day of 1979. We made the trip in an abandoned car I found in Maine and overhauled especially for the trek. I sold my CB radio to a trucker for gas money to complete the final leg of the journey. I had thoughts like *This time it'll be different. I'm going to turn over a new leaf.* I meant it with every fiber of my being...

The original plan was for Kandy and I to stay with one of her relatives who had a home north of Los Angeles until I got a job and got on my feet. When we reached our destination and pulled into the driveway, Kandy got out of the car, grabbed her bags, said good-bye, and promptly walked into the home. I was stunned at being left to find my way in unfamiliar surroundings. I drove to Anaheim to talk to one of her sisters, not knowing what else to do. I finally landed in Costa Mesa, and after a friend in Maine wired me a hundred dollars to get by, I got a job at the local Pep Boys as a "tire buster."

After a couple of weeks of working and sleeping in the car, one of my coworkers invited me to share his apartment down the street from where we worked. In a short time, I was drinking and smoking dope again but was responsible enough to set aside money to pay my share of the rent and utilities. Twice a week I'd make the one-hour trip to see Kandy, even though the visits were awkward.

Over the course of a few months, I worked my way up from being a tire installer to a mechanic as I started to purchase tools and eventually became the shop foreman. My roommate was fired for thievery and moved out of the apartment. I was surprised to discover from the apartment manager that he was three months behind on the rent, even though I'd given him my half every month! I found out one night that even the utility bills weren't paid when I came home to a pitch black apartment. The manager was kind enough, however, to let me move into a smaller, cheaper two-bedroom apartment, giving me an opportunity to catch up on the rent. I found a second job at a Denny's in Anaheim as a bartender to supplement my income.

Kandy asked me at one point if she could move back in with me, and I enthusiastically agreed. I was able to help her land employment at the restaurant I worked at. I thought all was going well for next three months, until Kandy came and told me one afternoon, "John, I love you, but I'm no longer *in* love with you... I think we should see other people."

I moved into the spare bedroom, feeling like the kiss of death had been given to me, but I decided to live with it because I thought she would eventually change her mind. One evening, I was sitting in the living room drinking wine and feeling sorry for myself. Kandy was leaving to go out on a date, and I vaguely remember muttering something to the effect that she'd never looked that good when we went somewhere. One thing led to another, and as she closed the door to go, I lost it and threw the gallon bottle of wine at the door in a rage. When she came home two days later, I apologized for my outburst and promised that it wouldn't happen again.

I secretly decided to give Kandy what I thought was a dose of her own medicine and started going out to bars, trolling for other women. I met a woman and started dating her without mentioning the fact that I had a roommate. A few weeks later, I announced that I was taking my new friend Kim to the Colorado River for the weekend. I returned Monday morning, and as I started up the stairs to the apartment, I immediately felt a sense of dread. At the top of the landing, I saw the front door ajar and slowly went in only to find a "Dear John" letter on the kitchen table. Through the tears streaming down my face, I read how Kandy couldn't take it anymore and had decided to fly home to Cleveland.

The next few weeks were a blur because I was so emotionally crushed. I used and abused everything I could get my hands on to numb the pain inside. I'd never taken the time to look at the part I played in driving her away from me...

Months later, after pulling myself together as best I could, I moved into a run-down hotel to conserve money (actually, I was evicted from the apartment) and started going to the gym, trying my best to look good on the outside while vaguely hoping that it would help to heal my insides. I soon felt enough self-esteem to try dating again and met Monica at one of the local dance clubs.

Monica and I dated for a few months, and we eventually married. I was living the life of a yuppie in southern California during the early eighties. I thought that I'd found a bright spot in my seemingly dull "life stone," and, paradoxically, was so blinded by it that it almost destroyed me. I had pride in the fact that I was now a Jaguar technician, and Monica was a legal secretary. If you were on the outside looking in, our life seemed normal in every respect. We had lots of friends and went out socializing with people while living in a two-bedroom townhouse in Huntington Beach.

The lies and secretive behavior on my part started soon after we were married because of the enigma dwelling in our home. Although I didn't realize it at the time, the entities lurking in our home were the diseases of alcoholism and addiction that began to reveal themselves after years of taunting. I began to justify my increasing drug use by rationalizing that *she doesn't need to know about the bonuses or side-job money I'm getting because I deserve this as a reward for my hard work.*

In 1981, we purchased a home, a new BMW, and all of the other trappings I thought were necessary to make our lives complete. Twisted awareness made me think that I was being a responsible husband by "bringing home the bacon," remodeling and repainting the inside of our new home, building a backyard fence, and landscaping the small property. Monica would deposit my paycheck every week but didn't know that I was tapping the ATM for my "recreational" cocaine use. The truth about my behavior came to light when the mortgage holders wanted to repossess our home for lack of payment. I suddenly found myself trapped like a rat, and for the first time in my life, I told the reality as I then knew it—I had a cocaine problem. Monica tried to support me and insisted I get some help for my problem. And so I promised to make things right...

For the next few months, I worked overtime and performed side jobs to raise the money necessary to get back on track. I got help by talking to Barbara, a marriage counselor we'd been seeing from almost day one; she was also an addiction specialist. I sincerely wanted with all my heart to repair the damage I had done to my relationship with Monica. Not knowing the true nature of the beast that I was dealing with, I tried hypnosis therapy for a period of time without any lasting effect. Although the financial damage was eventually repaired, the emotional devastation I caused in our home got worse every time I started using again. A family friend, in recovery himself, introduced me to the programs of Narcotics Anonymous and Cocaine Anonymous.

For the next five years, I went to a CA meeting once a week, often under the influence of something other than cocaine, thinking the entire time that I was okay. Regulars at the meeting would patiently try to explain to me that sobriety involved a lifestyle without *any* mind-altering substances, but the idea never got through. I often tried to play the "good boy" act for a period of time, and eventually all hell would break loose when I'd go on a drug and alcohol induced binge that always included infidelity and some other sort of shady behavior.

Somehow, while going to that weekly meeting, a seed got planted and began to take root... I endured a kind of personal hell I wouldn't wish on my worst enemy. I *knew* that something was wrong with me but didn't have any idea what it was. I was miserable most of the time with the constant thought that I was just taking up space while sucking someone else's air, and despite all of the "things" I'd acquired, I was still a complete failure. I began to have a vague feeling that my destiny was to slip into unconsciousness one day and never wake up, and I actually became okay with the idea...

For a short while, I found a diversion that lifted me out of my misery when I came across an old sun-faded and dusty Fiat 124 Spider in the back lot where I worked. I asked my boss, Buzz, about it and was told that the owner couldn't pay for the repairs, so Buzz ended up with it. I offered to buy it for a hundred dollars, even though it had been sitting for years. I bought it from him and started a restoration project that kept me out of trouble as I lovingly rebuilt it from the ground up. The little hot rod became my pride and joy.

In the spring of 1986, my father had a heart attack. Monica and I flew to Maine to be with him. When we got to the hospital, the sight of my father shook me to my core. The man that I'd always looked up to—and secretly looked down on with contempt—was helplessly lying in a bed, frail and scared. I started on an unwitting suicide mission that included drinking and using any drugs available to put myself into a state of oblivion... Monica stayed for a week as I postponed going back to California for another two weeks until my father came home from the hospital. Monica was infuriated when she picked me up at LAX as I poured out of the plane in a drunken stupor.

The next six months were a fog because I was usually under the influence of something to cover up or bury my feelings of uselessness and self-loathing. The only solace I found during that self-imposed suffering was in the work I did, so I often toiled late into the night to avoid talking to anyone. Even that started to change as I slipped further into the dark depths of untreated alcoholism and drug addiction.

Monica finally reached her breaking point one night in October 1986 after an explosive argument and told me to get out of the house. A sleeping bag up in the loft over the garage I worked at served as a refuge for the next three weeks. Fleeting moments of clarity started to creep into my consciousness as I went through the motions at work. On a Friday morning I called Monica, telling her that I was out of control, that I didn't want to cause her any more pain, and that maybe it was time we got a divorce.

The next few days were a "brownout," because the binge I started was like no other. It wasn't the worst one I ever went on, but the end resulted in an experience I'd never had before because of the way it got my attention. After the shop closed, I barricaded myself in the garage drinking, snorting, and smoking everything I could find, perhaps trying to fulfill my secret death wish. By 5:00 a.m. on Sunday I was out of booze, out of dope, and out of options. While splashing some cold water on my face in the bathroom, I happened to glance into the mirror, and in the span of a nanosecond, I got an unhindered look at my entire life up until that moment, and I couldn't stomach what I saw…

Something happened to the perceptions I had of myself when experiencing a sliver of clarity so up close and personal. I never had any intention of becoming the kind of man I was at that time, consumed by so many forms of selfishness and grandiosity, hurting everyone near and dear to me. I felt lonelier than I ever thought possible. I vaguely remember hitting my knees and crying while asking God to help me.

I managed to make it to the desk in the front office while shaking and sobbing for what seemed like hours. I somehow found Barbara's business card in my wallet. It had her home number on it. I called, waking her at the crack of dawn, telling her that I couldn't do it anymore and asking her for help. This was the first time in my life I followed someone's direction, no questions asked…

It took a couple of hours to pull myself together enough to drive to the home I'd just been thrown out of. I got some clothes together and asked Monica if she would take me to the hospital

Barbara told me to go to for their twenty-eight day treatment program. That was on November 2, 1986. I didn't know anything about treatment and had no idea what was in store for me. After two days of sleeping through most of my detox phase, I awoke to the sight of a couple of marshals accompanied by the director of the chemical dependency unit. The marshals were there to serve me with divorce papers. My life as I then knew it was coming to an end, and with a sigh of resignation, I signed the paperwork, going back to my bed feeling numb through and through.

The next day, I was feeling physically well enough that the staff decided it was time for me to get acquainted with what was expected of me while in their unit. The first thing, aside from the daily curriculum, was the requirement that I attend AA meetings. I thought I was a pretty smart guy knowing what NA and CA were, but what was AA? When they told me "Alcoholics Anonymous," I was confused. I didn't have a problem with alcohol, so what was the deal with that? But with another sigh of resignation, I agreed with their conditions, only because I was willing to do whatever I was told...

It is a strange, curious phenomenon that as soon as an alcoholic or addict feels physically better, his or her ego immediately recovers, as mine did. Even though I'd checked into the hospital for a month of treatment, I felt that I had to go after only three or four days. I had gotten a rest, and, after all, I was in charge of the shop, and I knew they wouldn't be able to get along without me. I was fortunate that a kind physician, recognizing what a serious problem I had, took the time to talk to me and convinced me to stay until the end of the week in hopes that I might "get it."

A few days later, I had my first exposure to Alcoholics Anonymous, and a "light bulb" came on. When I entered the meeting room, a person came up to me, gave me a hug, and whispered into my ear, "Welcome home." What a strange bunch these people were! The speaker that night was, in my mind, a stereotypical alcoholic. He looked a few hours older than dirt and decrepit (he kind of resembled the character Yoda in the *Star Wars* movies). He introduced himself as Bill H., a "real alcoholic." I was convinced that he couldn't tell me anything of importance and wondered what a "real alcoholic" was. Did that mean there were fake alcoholics or generic alcoholics? Bill didn't tell me anything that night—instead I "heard" a lot of questions asked, the first being "Have you ever been in a roomful of people and felt like the loneliest person on the planet?" My jaw dropped. How did he know?

Typically, every person coming into a 12-Step meeting for the first time arrives carrying a denial mechanism often referred to as "terminal uniqueness" because he or she thinks they're so different, and my exclusivity almost killed me. As Bill continued with his talk, I heard obvious questions like, "Did you ever go to the bar or to the dope boy and say you were only going to have one and never have it happen that way?" and "Did you ever wake up in strange places—with strange people?" I still don't know to this day if Bill actually asked those questions, but that's what I "heard," and it got my attention so quickly, it almost gave me whiplash. Somehow, during the course of Bill's talk that Friday night, the glare of the facets of twisted perceptions I suffered from dissipated long enough for me to finally relate. At the end of the meeting, it took everything I could muster to shake his hand and mumble a polite "thank you." I rode in the white van back to the hospital that night thinking that maybe there was something to this "AA stuff" after all.

The next day I found myself begging Polly P., the director of the chemical dependency unit, to let me stay the whole twenty-eight days because I had a change of heart...

Note: I never took the opportunity to thank Bill for carrying what was to be a life-saving message to my ears that evening. Even though I attended some of the same meetings that he did, my shattered and pulverized self-esteem wouldn't allow me to approach him. What is truly baffling to me to this day is that I've heard several tapes of his talks, and not once did he ask any of the questions that I "heard" at my first AA meeting. Whatever station or channel my "antenna" was tuned into ultimately sent me on a journey like no other. Additionally, I knew that Barbara was an addiction specialist but didn't realize it until later that she was also a thirty-year sober member of Alcoholics Anonymous. Years later she said that she started to "save me a seat" the first time we met for marriage counseling but had to let me run to the end of my rope...

Chapter 2
The Glare Begins to Lessen Just a Bit

After being assured by Polly that I could stay for the entire month, I called Buzz to let him know that I was going to be in the hospital for the next three weeks. One of Monica's many valid complaints about me was that I could never keep a job. I always had the arrogant attitude that I had never been unemployed more than two hours. After being sober for a while and looking back, I finally realized that during the first half of our six-year marriage, I had several different jobs. I'd been working for Buzz for three years by the time I checked in for treatment. Although Buzz initially came across as a gruff and ill-tempered kind of employer, he reluctantly told me to get well as soon as possible so that I could get back to work...

Note: I didn't know it at the time, but two days earlier, Buzz was approached at the shop by a dope dealer wanting to collect the money I owed him. Without hesitation, Buzz paid the man in full and told him never to come back again and contact me, or the police would be called. He, of course, was repaid in installments when I came back to work. Buzz's kindness still touches me to this day...

  I immediately began to immerse myself in the daily group sessions with the other seventeen patients and the counselors running them. Polly assigned Ginny B. as my primary counselor to work with me one-on-one in order to help address issues that were sure to surface as the treatment process continued. The first concern was my physical well-being. I'm 6'2" and weighed only 163 pounds when I checked into the hospital. Cocaine addicts usually have no desire for food when they are using, and their bodies pay for it. So, understandably, I found it difficult at first to consume three meals a day.
  Ginny gave me a copy of the book *Alcoholics Anonymous,* suggesting I read the first 164 pages because it was the text and the instructions for the 12-Step program I was going to need to learn and apply in my life in order to achieve long-term recovery. Every spare moment I had during the next

few weeks would find me with my face between the pages of the book, trying to decipher its meaning. Although I could understand what I read as I was reading it, I couldn't tell you what I read ten minutes after I put the book down. Normally, I could read an automotive shop manual from cover to cover and retain it all, but it felt like I was reading a foreign language when it came to trying to digest the material in the Big Book (AA's fond nickname for the book *Alcoholics Anonymous*). I kept reading it over and over, even though it didn't make sense to me at the time.

There were many discussions during group sessions about what was called the "disease concept" of alcoholism and drug addiction. I found the idea much easier to understand when a counselor used the term "dis-ease," because it described how I felt most of my life. Years earlier, I recalled thinking that I was leading a life of "quiet desperation." What was I so desperate for? That became one of the many questions running through my mind during the quiet times in my hospital room.

Thursday nights were considered "Family Night," because spouses, family members, and those close to the patients were invited to participate in group therapy sessions facilitated by a counselor. Monica came during the second week of my stay in treatment and sat in the circle of participants with her arms folded, understandably unresponsive during the gathering, seething with hostility. Afterward, we went to my room to talk privately and she began a venomous onslaught about how I'd emotionally abused her and our relationship for years, and I was now "hiding out" on vacation rather than taking responsibility for the damage I'd caused. We were definitely getting a divorce, and our house was going to be sold as a result of it. Words like "loser" and the term "selfish bastard" kept popping up during the course of the one sided exchange. I sat there sullenly, not saying a word, knowing I didn't have a leg to stand on because everything that came out of her mouth was absolutely true, with the exception of me "hiding out" on vacation, but even then, I didn't have it in me to voice an objection. After she left, I laid in my bed with tears of sorrow and remorse silently trickling onto the pillow until I finally fell asleep early the next morning.

Friday morning found me with swollen red eyes, looking like I always did after a night of drinking and using, sitting in a group preoccupied with the events of the last evening when I was called to Polly's office. She informed me that my insurance would only cover two weeks of treatment, so Sunday was going to have to be my last day. She sensed something in my reaction that prompted her to make an arrangement with me to complete the program. Polly suggested that if I were willing enough to be there promptly at 7:00 a.m. every morning, to attend all of the group sessions as well as a 12-Step meeting every evening, she'd allow me to participate and complete the remaining two weeks of treatment. I agreed to her terms.

Later that day, I summoned up enough courage to call Monica and ask if I could sleep in one of the other bedrooms until I completed the program. Sunday afternoon, she picked me up at the hospital and took me home to get my things in order. I went through all of my hiding places in the house, the garage, and my car, removing all of the paraphernalia and destroying anything associated with my drug use.

The next morning, after spending the night on the futon in the spare bedroom, I drove to the hospital, arriving twenty minutes early so I wouldn't miss out on anything. The first group of the day included a video about cocaine addiction. The narrator stated that possibly three out of a hundred addicts would stay sober for anything close to a year. Hearing that, I found myself looking around the room, wondering who the other two people would be. Something began to stir deep within my psyche—a want of something other than what I'd been experiencing up to the date I checked into treatment...

During the next two weeks, I went to all of the required group therapy sessions. Between sessions, I often went to a storage room, where I found an old recliner to sit in by myself and voraciously read my Big Book, trying to make sense of it all.

At the end of the day, I would go to my estranged home to take a shower, change clothes, and go to an AA meeting. The mood upon entering the house was always on edge as Monica and I avoided engaging in any exchange other than strained small talk. The only significant conversations we had during that time were when we contacted a real estate agent to put the house up for sale and how to expedite the deal. In order to even begin making amends to the woman I'd emotionally abused for so long, I signed a quick claim deed, handing over my interest in the house to Monica.

I experienced "being of service" for the first time during the Thanksgiving holiday. The hospital cafeteria staff prepared hundreds of turkey sandwiches to be delivered to "skid row" in Los Angeles. The treatment staff and patients piled themselves and the sandwiches into a couple of vans and cars driving to the downtown area. As we made our way to the shelter, I noticed the cardboard boxes lining the sidewalks where people slept every night. When we got to the shelter, we set up shop and started to pass out the sandwiches and drinks. After everyone had a chance to eat, an impromptu AA meeting started. One by one, people started to share about how grateful they were that someone cared enough to bring them a Thanksgiving meal. As the meeting progressed, I experienced a panic attack. I started to shake, remembering a time in my life that I'd completely blocked out—in 1974 I was living on the streets in Baltimore for a short time when I was seventeen years old and running from the law. Ginny held me in her arms, trying to console me as the meeting went on.

One man shared about how grateful he was that he didn't steal as much as he used to now that he was six months sober. I couldn't come close to understanding how somebody would be grateful for that! Ginny reminded me that the 12-Step way of life is a "program of progress and not perfection." At the beginning of our trip to skid row, I had an attitude of "being better than" those people living on the streets. Once I saw the reality of what they lived in, and in reliving my experience on the streets, my way of thinking started the tedious journey of making a 180-degree shift. I unknowingly began to develop an "attitude of gratitude" that would save me when I least expected it.

"We admitted that we were powerless over alcohol—that our lives had become unmanageable."
(Step 1 of Alcoholics Anonymous)

Something was subtly different about the AA meetings I attended every night as compared with the CA meeting I went to once a week for the five years prior to treatment. It took some time for me to realize that the meetings themselves were not different—I was. The subject matter of both 12-Step meetings was, in fact, the same; getting a sponsor, working the steps, developing a relationship with a Higher Power, and so on. For the first time, I was really listening and trying to absorb what was being discussed during the meetings. And I asked a lot of questions. My questions led me to a couple of old-timers who helped me begin to make sense of what I kept reading.

They went out of their way to make it abundantly clear to me that the only thing I had to do perfectly in this program was to take the first step without any reservations whatever. They assured me that if I managed that and did the best I could, I'd be okay with the rest of the steps. The older crusty gentlemen said that I was trying too hard to follow directions. Although I was following through on the suggestions given me by reading the first 164 pages, since I started at page one, going to page 164, I was "missing the boat." The veterans pointed out to me that the most important part of the book came immediately before page one. It's a chapter titled "The Doctor's Opinion." I was told that if I didn't understand and grasp the concepts discussed in the chapter, I was wasting my time with the rest of the book. The chapter explains the "nature of the beast," as they put it. They took the liberty of giving me my very first reading assignment with specific directions—I was told to read the chapter and look for the term "phenomenon of craving," and every time I came across it to highlight it and really think about how or if it applied to me.

Although I didn't know it at the time, I was suffering from an ailment called "selective listening," because I was still thinking with the mind of a cocaine addict (because I was different than the drunks trying to help me), not realizing that I had a problem with alcohol as well. I read the chapter highlighting what I was told to, and when I came to the last example of that term, I used my own interpretation when reading it. The sentence says, "These and many others have one symptom in common, they cannot start drinking without developing the phenomenon of craving." I honestly thought it said, "they cannot start drinking without developing the phenomenon of craving *for more alcohol.*" One of the guys kindly pointed out to me where the period is at the end of the sentence. This was the very first time I heard the expression "read the black on the page," because I had to read the chapter three or four more times before they were satisfied that I finally understood what was being talked about.

Frank H. (Bill H.'s brother) then told me something that saved my life. "John, I really don't care what your deal is. If you have a drink of alcohol, and let's say you suddenly develop a craving to do something strange with a farm animal, or you might develop a craving to do some of that white stuff you're always talking about, or smoke dope, chase women, hang out in bars, run scams on people, or even commit armed robbery, I don't care. Here's the deal: if you have a drink of alcohol and you have a craving of any kind for anything, guess what?" He told me that I was "a dead, stinking fish."

Later, in the quiet darkness of my room, I closely examined my relationship with alcohol, taking everything else I had been doing out of the equation. The old codger was right. I opened my Big Book and looked at a sentence early in the chapter that says "these allergic types can never safely use alcohol in any form at all." The one thing that I learned while in treatment is that alcohol is a drug. It is the oldest drug known to man. I used to mistakenly think that it was a stimulant, but actually it's a sedative that happens to be in liquid form. The term "alcohol in any form and all" suddenly started to click. The sentence was also talking about the dope I smoked or snorted, the pills I popped, and even the model airplane glue I sniffed at one point in my life. Two and two finally added up to four!

I finally understood the concept of powerlessness when I took a drink or a drug. The second half of the step was still confusing to me. Although my wife had thrown me out of the house, I technically was still married, I still had the house, the cars, all my bills were paid, and I wasn't in danger of losing my job. So what did "our lives had become unmanageable" mean? One of the men at a meeting was able to clear it up for me by asking a question. He asked, "Have you ever been getting ready to do something, it doesn't matter what it was, and you had a voice in the back of your mind saying, 'John, what you're getting ready to do is wrong—don't do it!' And you did it anyway? That's unmanageability." I thought about the fact that my parents taught me how it was wrong to lie, cheat, and steal, yet I found myself doing those things, knowing full well somewhere in the back of my mind that it really was morally wrong, but I did it anyway. At this point, I was able to digest and get a grasp of the full impact of the first step. I've always found it interesting that chapters one, two, and three are all directly related to the first step. Do you think that somebody's trying to make a point?

Note: I've always given the new guys I work with the same first reading assignment. I never chase them down to see if it's done or not—I ask them to call me when they've got it completed as a way of showing me how willing they are. It often takes several times of going through the chapter and having the same conversation that Frank did with me before I'm confident that the newcomer understands and accepts the first step for what it really is. One of the things I love doing is, whether I'm at a first step table at a meeting or even a detox center, explaining and "breaking down" everything in "The Doctor's Opinion" the way it was done for me because the guys who patiently worked with me in those early days made it so much easier to understand and accept.

During the last week of treatment, Ginny suggested that I find a sponsor who would help me out with the steps. I had a relationship with one of the male counselors and asked him to be my "temporary sponsor." Tony had been sober for a period of time, and his motto was "if you use, you lose." How true this is for a person trying to recover and has a go at it one more time. During one of the many conversations I had with him, I brought up my concerns about the ninth step because I knew I was going to have to make amends to my soon to be ex-wife about my many indiscretions during our marriage. Tony reminded me that the step has an important qualifier, "except when to do so would injure them or others." He said that I wasn't at that step yet, and an amends to Monica might cause more harm than good, so it might be something I'd have to sit on for the rest of my life. Tony then said, "And besides, God will give you a sign if the step is indicated." That gave me some relief.

December 2, 1986 was filled with lots of anxiety, since it was my last day in treatment. I knew I was going back to work in an area where there was lots of alcohol and drug use, and it scared me. I was assured by Polly, Ginny, and Tony that if I went to work, went to a meeting every day, and asked my Higher Power for help, I'd be okay.

I was at work the next day with so much to do that the thought of a drink or drug didn't even occur to me. I worked hard the next few weeks, catching up on everything that had piled up at the shop. There was one particular vehicle that I had to address immediately. A Jaguar XJS had suffered a catastrophic failure that required the upper half of its twelve-cylinder engine to be removed. My selfish and greedy nature showed itself because I only worked on the quick and easy money making repairs that didn't need a lot of effort. Because of this, the car stayed outside baking in the southern California sunshine for over five months before I removed a bolt from it. The customer would call every ten days or so, looking for a status report, and I would lie with any kind of story I could dream up to placate the man who put his trust in my abilities.

By the time the car made it into the shop, the paint was so cracked and faded that I told Buzz I would pay for a repaint after the repair work was done. The repair was tedious, as well as time-consuming—I went out of my way to resist the urge to work on the quick "in and out" jobs until the motor was done and purred like a kitten. I also found a number of little leaks the car had because of its prolonged stay in one spot. When the customer called once again for an update, I was honest with him and told him of my plans to repaint the car for him and fix the minor leaks at my expense, which greatly relieved him.

I started to enjoy going to those "A and A" meetings because they helped reduce the tensions of the day. Someone in one of the meetings I attended suggested that mild exercise would also help with any anxiety or frustrations I might have. I was already a member of a gym, so I started some weight training and jogging.

I soon had a routine that included either jogging or going to the gym in the morning before going to work. After a full day of work, I would race to the house that had a "For Sale" sign planted in the front lawn to put some time into whatever project I was doing before going to an evening meeting.

At about forty-five days of sobriety, I was given an up-close and personal look at me as an example of exactly how selfish and self-centered I was. I came home from a meeting that night and found Monica sitting on the couch, and I could tell that she was pissed off. You could cut the tension in the air with a knife. When I asked her what was wrong, she presented me with a business card that she found on the floorboard of my car and said, "I found this in your car and was curious about the women's names and phone numbers listed on the back of the card. So I called one of these numbers and got a pretty interesting story. Would you care to tell me about it?"

In my twisted mind, I thought, *Oh my God, this must be the sign that Tony was telling me about.* I proceeded to tell Monica about that indiscretion, as well as every other episode of infidelity I'd committed while we were married. She began to cry, and soon she was sobbing uncontrollably. When I finished, she told me that none of the phone numbers were called—she was just fishing. I was mortified because I realized that I was guilty of trying to save my own skin at Monica's expense. The last thing in the world I wanted to do was cause her more harm, and that's exactly what I did. It wasn't until a year and a half later that I was able to truly make amends to her for actions that included my inept first attempt.

The next day I went to the treatment center looking for Tony. When I told him about how badly I screwed up the night before, he said that the steps were numbered and in a specific order for a reason. I had no business even attempting what I did, despite what I thought was a "sign," without taking the previous eight steps. He then asked me a question: "What do you get when you sober up a horse thief?" Without even giving me a chance to think about it, Tony raised his voice and said, "You get a sober horse thief!" He then explained that the steps were designed to help a person not only change his or her way of thinking, but more importantly, their behavior. Even though I wasn't drinking or using drugs, Tony told me that I would remain a "sober horse thief" until I took the steps in order and applied them into my life. He told me to find a permanent sponsor and start going through the steps in the Big Book.

In hindsight, I now know that it was no coincidence I came across the man who would be my first sponsor the following Friday night in La Palma. Buck M. was six or seven years sober at the time and was the speaker at the meeting I adopted as my "home group." He was full of energy and had a kind of laugh that I hadn't heard in years. After the meeting, everyone usually went to the Denny's restaurant down the street to have coffee and dessert. I joined the crowd, eventually getting up enough courage to sheepishly approach Buck and ask him if we could talk for a minute. I swallowed my pride, quietly telling him about my situation and my need for help. After beating around the bush for a while, I finally asked him if he would be my sponsor. Buck told me that some ground rules needed to be laid out from the start if he was going to help me. He first of all assured me that he would never ask me to do anything that he hadn't done himself. Everything he did was right out of the Big Book. He then asked, "Based on that premise, are you willing to do whatever it takes to stay sober?" I thought to myself, *If it works for him, maybe it'll work for me.* I agreed and started the most difficult journey of my life, and it was only eighteen inches long—from my head to my heart...

Note: It's because of Buck that today I lay out the same ground rules to men asking for my help...

As time went on, people began to think of me as Buck's shadow at the meetings we went to together. Buck couldn't turn around without bumping into me. We soon became friends and discovered many common interests. Buck and I were both avid skiers and would often make the two-hour drive up a mountain to spend a day and early evening on the slopes. One of the many things that I loved about southern California was that you could surf (I was starting to learn how to do that with my buddy, Tom W.) in the morning and go skiing in the afternoon. Buck would often give me reading assignments in the Big Book and also told me to take notes, use a dictionary, and ask any questions coming to mind. During one of our many conversations, my sponsor asked me how many different kinds of alcoholics there were. Having recently gotten out of a treatment center, armed with all of this newfound knowledge on the subject, I proceeded to explain the Type 1 and Type 2 when he abruptly stopped me and said, "John there's only three kinds: a practicing alcoholic, a sober alcoholic, and a dead alcoholic—what kind do you want to be?"

Chapter 3
Looking Good on the Outside but Dying on the Inside

"Came to believe that a Power greater than ourselves could restore us to sanity."
(Step 2 of Alcoholics Anonymous)

I had difficulty with understanding the second step because I thought an inference was being made that I was a nutcase and needed a rubber room. In an exercise done in group while in treatment, I wrote down what was called a "jackpot list" to help examine my behavior. I saw in black and white that every single time I had some difficulty in my life, alcohol and dope was always in the equation. I also saw that when I was involved in some sort of shady behavior, I honestly thought I was going to get away with it. It was pointed out to me that this could be construed as a form of insanity itself. I began to understand that the insanity of the alcoholic occurs when he or she is "stone cold sober" and makes the decision to pick up the first drink one more time.

After reading the fourth chapter in the Big Book, entitled "We Agnostics" (this chapter is entirely devoted to the second step), I went to Buck more confused than ever about the "Higher Power" thing. Sure, I was raised as a Catholic, did the altar boy gig, but could never come to grips with the idea of a loving and all-powerful God. At that point in my life, I was convinced that God looked exactly like Charlton Heston from the movie *The Ten Commandments* and was standing on a dark mountaintop with a lightning bolt in his hand, waiting to zap me and turn me into a French fry the next time I screwed up. Where I got this notion, I still have no idea.

Buck patiently asked me to set aside my preconceived notions for the time being and referred me to page 47 of the text, where a question appears: "Do I now believe, or am I even willing to believe, that there is a power greater than myself?" I was told that the question only required a yes-or-no answer. My response was a cautious "Yeah, but..."

At this point, Buck simplified things by asking, "Do you believe that I believe?" I thought to myself, *He obviously believes in something because it's working for him.* "Yes, I do," I replied, starting from below "ground zero" with a willingness to believe that Buck believed opened a door that I didn't know existed. As time went by, I learned that the first three words, "Came to believe," indicate that the second step is a process, and we don't necessarily have to get "zapped" to fully take the step: the only thing required is willingness.

Note: Just as untreated alcoholism and addiction are "equal opportunity destroyers," a 12-Step program applied with enough willingness can be an "equal opportunity restorer."

     This newly acquired willingness to believe in something other than myself had a test during my first sober Christmas holiday. I was finished with all of the repairs and upgrades on the house. Although divorce proceedings were started, Monica and I were getting along as best we could. My youngest brother Lucien (everyone called him "Pee-Wee") came to visit over the holiday. Monica suggested that we all go to Lake Arrowhead to visit her parents and have dinner on Christmas Eve with the two of them. I reluctantly went along with the idea, so we piled into the BMW and drove to the mountains.

     Joe, Monica's father, was a man that I looked up to and had a pretty good relationship with. The two of us spent some time talking privately on the porch, where I tried to apologize for being such a jerk to his daughter. He told me that things happen during a marriage, and I should really focus my apologies on Monica.

     During dinner that evening, the conversation around the table somehow got to the subject of mistakes that people make. Monica commented on what a mistake she made marrying me in the first place. She then started telling her parents about the times I was unfaithful to her. The more she elaborated on my infidelities, the more embarrassed I got. With face flushed red and burning with shame, I excused myself, got up from the table, and went outside.

     In the frigid night air, I sat on the bumper of my car and cried. For the first time in almost two months, I wanted to get loaded more than ever. My brother came out to console me and asked if there was anything he could do. I explained to Pee-

Wee through my tears that everything Monica said at the dinner table was true, and I felt as if a knife had been stuck in my gut and was being twisted for all it was worth.

While I was talking to my brother, we heard the peal of a church bell that sounded as if it were just down the street. If you've ever been in the mountains late at night during the wintertime, you'd know that sounds carry for miles. I suggested that we take a drive and find out where the sound was coming from. We drove about five miles with a window rolled down, following the sound of the distant bell, and discovered a little church preparing to celebrate Midnight Mass. I hadn't been to a church in years and suggested that we go in. As Pee-Wee and I sat in the back row of the congregation, I started to feel a calm come over me. It wasn't anything I could put my finger on, but the overwhelming urge to get loaded was gone. After the church service, we drove back to the house, where all was dark and quiet because everyone was asleep. We said goodnight to each other and went to bed.

During the drive down the mountain the next day, not a word was said. When we got home, Pee-Wee packed his things for his return flight to Maine. He said good-bye to Monica, and I drove him to the airport. As he was getting ready to board his plane, I gave him a hug and thanked him for saving my bacon the night before.

When the holidays were over, I went to visit Ginny and talked at length to her about what happened on Christmas Eve. I tried to explain how the calmness came over me that night in the church but couldn't find the words for it. I couldn't articulate how badly I wanted this thing. I was struggling with the "Higher Power" idea and knew it would prevent me from ever "getting it." Even though I really believed that Buck believed, it felt as if the entire concept was still beyond my grasp, and it frustrated me to no end. I heard in meetings about what eventually happened to people who didn't have a "Higher Power" in their lives. Ginny smiled and asked me to follow her. We went to the classroom I had sat in four times a day for my month of treatment. She calmly pointed to a poster on the wall, asking me to read it to myself. It contained the poem titled "Footprints in the Sand," and as I started to read it, a tear started to trickle down my cheek…

Footprints in the Sand

One night I dreamed I was walking along the beach with the Lord.
Many scenes from my life flashed across the sky.
In each scene I noticed footprints in the sand.
Sometimes there were two sets of footprints,
other times there were one set of footprints.

This bothered me because I noticed
that during the low periods of my life,
when I was suffering from
anguish, sorrow or defeat,
I could see only one set of footprints.
So I said to the Lord,
"You promised me Lord,
that if I followed you,
you would walk with me always.
But I have noticed that during the most trying periods of my life
there have only been one set of footprints in the sand.
Why, when I needed you most, you have not been there for me?"

The Lord replied,
"The times when you have seen only one set of footprints in the sand,
is when I carried you."

Anonymous

Perceptions, or lack thereof, are sometimes very curious, especially when something is right in front of you. The poster had been on the classroom wall the entire time I was in treatment, and yet I didn't "see" it. There is an old saying, "You can't see until you can see, and you can't hear until you can hear," and it certainly applied in this case. As I cried, Ginny hugged and comforted me, saying it was going to be okay. In that very instant, the wall of denial that had blocked me for so long started to crumble…

My memory flashed back to episodes in my life that I hadn't thought about in years: I was a seventeen-year-old sitting in my father's barn holding a revolver to my temple and not pulling the trigger; a car accident I walked away from in Baltimore while on the lam from the police in Maine; another accident in the Florida Everglades during a dope deal that should've killed me; getting beaten to a pulp after a drug deal went sour in Cleveland and making it out of town before a hit man found me. I'd have to be a fool to think there wasn't a Power greater than myself helping me survive these and many more dangerous situations I put myself in.

Note: When a man I'm working with gets to the second step, I always bring up the question in the Big Book that boils down the step to a yes-or-no answer and make it a point to ask him if he believes that I believe...

In early January 1987, the house was sold, and the process of moving out began. Monica found a small apartment in Newport Beach. One of my last remaining friends, Bob Gillespie, helped me move the furniture and anything else Monica wanted to her new place. I rented a storage area down the street from work to accommodate the remaining household items. As I was picking up the last few items in the house, I looked around with a deep sense of loss at the place I used to call home. I made the final trip to the storage area with a heavy heart.

I was once again spending my nights in a sleeping bag in the loft over the garage. By this time, I'd developed some stamina in my efforts at jogging. So I started a new routine. Every morning I would get up early and run about six miles. Fortunately, there was a shower stall at work, so I could get cleaned up before starting my job without smelling like a musty sock. At the end of the day, I would shower again, get dressed, have dinner somewhere, and go to a meeting. After the meeting, I would go to the gym, work out for a couple of hours, and retire to my sleeping bag for some much-needed rest. During my first few months of sobriety, I gained over fifty pounds, so I became obsessed with getting into shape. Along with this obsession came the need to look hip, slick, and cool to the people around me. I started to buy new clothes, trying to change my image and fit the new body I was sculpting by working out so hard and so often.

People at meetings started to call me "Jaguar John" because I usually drove a customer's Jag every evening in a vain effort to show everyone that I was okay and had it together. I was unknowingly doing what a lot of newcomers do, trying to fix everything on the outside, hoping that the inside would take care of itself. I often heard the expression "it's an inside job," but it went over my head at the time.

After I completed treatment, I began regularly attending an aftercare group on Tuesday nights, followed by an AA meeting in the same building. I was a little over three months sober when I met Sally, a patient in treatment at the time. She asked me if I'd look at her Honda that needed some minor repairs when she got out of treatment. I told her that I'd be more than happy to. Soon after she got out of treatment, I looked at her car, and within a short period of time, we started dating. Buck suggested to me that it wasn't a good idea to get involved in a new relationship during my first year of sobriety, and he followed that up with, "You can do anything you want to provided you're willing to pay the price." Needless to say, Sally and I were soon an item, and without realizing it, she started to become my higher power.

In February, Buzz told me that he and his family were going to visit his mother in South Africa for six weeks and asked if I would run the shop for him while he was gone. I was moved that Buzz would place his trust in me after the disruptions I caused. He also asked me to move into his home, watch over it, and tend to the pool while he was gone. I agreed, so we went to his bank to have my name added to the business account. I already knew the vendors Buzz used for parts, supplies, and everything else, including the labor rates he charged for specific jobs, so I felt prepared.

Sally would meet me over at Buzz's house after meetings, and we'd spend time watching videos and talking late into the night. I was really trying hard to do things right for once in my life, so I promised myself not to have sex with this woman until I got to know her.

As the day of Buzz's return approached, I felt satisfied with the job the entire staff had done. Not only had the workflow almost doubled, but all of Buzz's company bills were paid as well. I went over his house, making sure that it was cleaner than it had been when I moved in, and returned to my loft at the shop. Buzz took an entire day to go through the books and invoices before he called me into his office. He commended me on the work that we'd accomplished but admonished me for the way I had taken it upon myself to pay *all* of the bills because there wasn't enough of what he considered to be a prudent reserve or cash flow to fall back on. Buzz's observations about my lack of an ability to properly handle money would prove to be prophetic in the years to come.

After my divorce was finalized in April 1987, I flew to Maine for a week, bringing Sally along so she could meet my parents. I got an unfettered, sober look at myself as my mother dragged out the family photo album to share with Sally. Most of the holiday pictures with me in them usually showed me drunk or passed out someplace. While on the trip, Sally and I slept in separate hotel rooms, and it drove me crazy. The longer I went without having sex with her, the more I obsessed about it. Thankfully, that eased up a little when we returned to southern California.

I soon became friends with a group of guys at my home group roughly my age and with about the same length of sobriety. We used to hang out together after meetings and called ourselves the "road dogs" because we traveled together all over the area going to meetings.

One Friday night during the smoke break, we were hanging out in the parking lot. I was at the "I know" stage of my early recovery. When an old-timer would try to impart some words of wisdom to me, I always responded with "I know." I was approached that night by Ray G., a veteran of the group who had almost fifty years of sobriety. Ray smiled at me and said, "John, you seem to know an awful lot about this program."

Of course I replied, "I know..."

Ray asked, "Do you mind if I ask you a couple of questions?" I smiled and puffed up my chest, glancing at my "road dog" buddies and thinking to myself that I was going to be able to help this old guy by answering his questions.

I said, "Sure thing, Ray."

Ray said, "Why do you suppose that when a rabbit relieves itself, it comes out as pellets?"

I answered, "Gee, Ray, I don't know."

Ray then asked, "Why do you suppose that when a cow takes a dump, it comes out as a cow pie instead of a turd, like any other animal?" Again I replied that I didn't know.

Without blinking an eye, Ray responded with "Well, John, if you don't know shit, what makes you think you know anything about staying sober?" My friends howled and hooted with laughter while I felt extremely embarrassed.

I went to Buck, asking why an old codger like Ray was going out of his way to pick on me and embarrass me in front of my friends. Buck smiled and said, "He's not picking on you; he's trying to make a point, Grasshopper…You're working so hard at looking good on the outside, but I'll bet everything in my wallet that you're dying on the inside." I was astonished because my sponsor had pulled my covers and zeroed in on what was really going on. He had me pegged. One of the survival mechanisms I employed was to always look like I had it together and everything was okay. For the first time in my life, someone saw through the front I put up and called me on it. I was going through the motions with a huge hole inside and didn't know what to do about it.

I admitted the truth and told Buck that I was absolutely miserable. I asked what I could do to change things. He smiled again and said, "You can't think your way into better living; you have to live your way into better thinking." I hated it when he did that. My sponsor would always say things so simple and yet so profound that they would go over my head. Then I would have to humble myself and ask him what he meant by that. One of the things that used to really get me was when I started any sentence with the words "I think," and he would always interrupt me by asking who's scale of judgment I was using in whatever I was about to say. Of course, I would answer "mine," and it became a regular thing for him to remind me that my twisted thinking was what got me where I was in the first place, so perhaps I should stop relying on my "gray matter" for the time being.

Buck explained that it was time for me to get off my duff and start doing something different, like taking the steps and being of service. Taking the first two steps, coupled with a healthy dose of fear, would only work for so long. He went on to say that if I were to stay in the position I was in at that moment, the day would come when I would have only two options: to drink or to blow my brains out. Neither of those seemed attractive to me, so I got busy. I had my face back in my Big Book and started looking at the third step while getting an introduction to the first of many H&I (Hospitals & Institutions) committee meetings. I began to accompany Buck, as well as many other friends, going all over the southern California area, bringing meetings to people confined in hospitals, jails, and prisons.

"Made a decision to turn our will and our lives over to the care of God as we understood Him."
(Step 3 of Alcoholics Anonymous)

When reading about the third step (the bottom of page 60 to the top of page 64), I could finally relate to the descriptions in the Big Book about the guy who was always trying to run the show. He was like a chameleon, blending into whatever situation he found himself in. I'd always fancied myself as a true master manipulator because of the arsenal of strategies I had at my disposal. I could be kind and considerate, or on the other hand I could be hostile and step on peoples' toes to get what I wanted. I honestly thought everyone acted this way. I read about the six forms of self: selfishness, self-centeredness, self-delusion, self-pity, self-seeking, and fear that were described as character defects and became revolted at the possibility of having them myself. I went to Buck telling him that I didn't suffer from these character defects. He wryly smiled and said, "That's because, John, you don't have any character." I was crestfallen as he suggested that I highlight the forms of self and whether I thought they applied to me or not, because they would all come into play when I took my fourth step.

The first time I said the third step prayer, I was with my mentor in a parking lot outside of St. Anne's church in Seal Beach, just before the meeting began on a Thursday night.

There were almost a hundred people milling about that evening as Buck told me to open my Big Book to page 63 and read along with him as we recited the prayer on our knees. Something was different; for the first time in my life, I didn't care who saw me doing something "hokey." Afterward, he told me from that point on I was to start my day by hitting my knees, opening my book to that page, and reading that prayer out loud, verbatim, until it was "tattooed to my eyelids."

The next morning I was in a locked room, on my knees with an open book, reading a prayer I didn't understand to a God I didn't have a clue about, but I did it anyway because I knew that Buck did it too. *"God, I offer myself to Thee to build with me and to do with me as Thou wilt. Relieve me of the bondage of self, that I may better do Thy will. Take away my difficulties, that victory over them may bear witness to those I would help of Thy Power, Thy Love, and Thy Way of life. May I do Thy will always!"* Even though I felt like an idiot and was embarrassed to do it, I continued to force myself to recite the prayer every morning. Something started happening to me, though it wasn't apparent at first; micron by micron, my thinking started to change in spite of myself. As I verbalized the third step prayer, it began to take root and become internalized. This allowed me to start looking at the imperfections in the facets of my "life stone" without the intense glare of twisted perceptions and my blinded efforts at trying to rationalize (ration-of-lies) away my misguided behaviors.

Note: My understanding of the prayer is radically different today than what it was when I first started this journey. When I was new and reached the part of the prayer where I was asking God to "take away my difficulties," my mind would think about getting the wife back, the house and car back, having the bills paid off, and any other material thing you can think of. Being so self-absorbed at the time made it easy for me to ask God to give me back all the "stuff." The prayer doesn't have anything to do with things of a material nature at all.

Today when I'm asking Him to "take away my difficulties," I'm actually asking Him to let me be an example and stay sober, no matter what comes down the pike. We're all examples for somebody—directly or indirectly—and there's always someone watching us. The sad fact of the matter is that most of us are the perfect illustrations of what not to be doing. I might be the only example of the Big Book that someone sees, and there's no way on God's green earth that I can be that example without being knee-deep in the steps. That's why I have to ask Him to "relieve me of the bondage of self." There's no way I can help someone if all I'm doing is thinking about me.

There's an old proverb that simply asks, "How can you see the splinter in your friend's eye when there's a plank in your face?" Practicing the third step prayer on a daily basis has allowed me to set aside my plank so that I can be of service to someone...

Chapter 4
"I've Never Had It so Good"

After my trip to Maine, Dave, who owned an automotive repair shop next door to Buzz's place, offered me the use of his spare bedroom rent-free until I could get back on my feet again. Sleeping on a mattress on the floor was far better than the sleeping bag as far as I was concerned. Having access to Dave's washer and dryer was also much cheaper than going to the dry cleaners all the time. I also partnered up with Dave in a muffler shop venture to make extra money. I had a pile of bills to catch up on and pay off because I'd maxed out all of my credit cards while still using, and I had also used them to finance the trip to see my parents. Dave's kindness allowed me to see the light at the end of the tunnel when it came to the financial mess I had created for myself.

I soon found that there wasn't enough time during a twenty-four-hour period to fit in everything I wanted to accomplish. I remembered asking myself, while in treatment, about what I was going to do with all the spare time I'd have on my hands because I wasn't going to be drinking and using anymore. I ran every morning, worked all day, usually having lunch with Sally, went to a meeting every night, trained at the gym afterward, and crawled onto my mattress about midnight, only to wake up at 5:00 a.m. and start all over again. I didn't have the time to get loaded!

There was a short period in May 1987 when I didn't go to meetings for a couple of weeks. I took on so much work at the shop that I found myself putting in eighteen-hour days. I rationalized that because I had so many bills to pay, the quicker I got the jobs done, the sooner I would be out of debt. One afternoon, I got a call at work from one of the "road dogs," Marshall L., who asked me one question: "Are you drunk yet?" That was all I needed to hear, and I stopped the long days and started going to meetings again.

After getting back on track, I was planning to take Sally dancing at a nightclub I had frequented before I got sober. When I mentioned it to Buck, he looked at me and merely asked "What's your spiritual house like?" I looked back at him blankly, not understanding the point he was trying to make. Buck told me that if I didn't get what he was talking about, I had no business going to the club in the first place. I followed his advice and thankfully decided not to go.

A few days later, Sally and I were walking in the park across the street from the treatment center, having a heated discussion about why we weren't going dancing. I began to feel increasingly frustrated and started to think, *This is BS, why did I get sober and have to put up with this nonsense?* Then the lights went out, and I dropped to my knees. The very instant I had that negative thought, a Frisbee thrown from across the park hit me in the back of the neck, cold cocking me and causing me to see stars. For a while after that experience, every time I had a negative thought, even if I was in an enclosed room, I would look over my shoulder just in case a Frisbee was coming at me. My Higher Power definitely has a sense of humor.

Buzz allowed me to use the shop on Saturday mornings as a "car clinic" in order to help my newfound friends with minor auto repairs. They brought the parts needed with them, and I performed the repairs free of charge as a small way of being of service. I had begun to learn the meaning of altruism: doing something for somebody and expecting nothing in return. Up until that point, I never did anything for anybody without having the idea that something was in it for me. I'd been a taker all my life and was starting to make a few small changes...

On Saturday afternoons, I also volunteered to go to the treatment center where I had gotten sober to moderate an AA meeting for the patients. After one of these meetings, a patient named Alan R. asked me to be his sponsor. Without hesitation, I told Alan that I would be honored to. Later that afternoon, after thinking about the commitment I just made, I went to see Buck to ask him what I should do because I was only six months sober and hadn't taken all of the steps yet. Buck laughed and said, "Don't let him catch up with you." I smiled sheepishly and said okay, even though I was secretly betting money that Alan was going to get loaded a half hour after leaving treatment.

The first time I went to the Thursday night meeting at St. Anne's Church in Seal Beach, I encountered one of those crusty, ill-tempered long-timers named Fred P., who promptly told me to sit down and "pull the cotton out of my ears and put it in my mouth." In other words, I was told not too subtly to sit down and shut up. This annoyed me to no end, but I did it anyway. After finding out that I'd volunteered to be Alan's sponsor, Fred sought me out and started to poke me in the chest while telling me that I had no business sponsoring anyone until I had at least five years of sobriety. I've never heard Fred say that that to anyone else, but that's what I heard come from Fred's lips that night. The next day I introduced Alan to Buck, informing him that Buck was his new sponsor. Despite my early animosity toward Fred, we eventually became the best of friends.

Note: Alan passed away in December 2006, with over nineteen years of sobriety.

Almost every Thursday night, I would be accosted by my friend Frank H., the elder statesman who always asked me how my fourth step was coming along. Every week I would mutter the same answer: "I'm working on it Frank, I'm working on it..." This made me uncomfortable because I couldn't look Frank in the eye when I answered. The truth was that I wasn't working on it at all although I did spent a lot of time thinking about it. At about six and a half months of sobriety, after receiving the same standard answer from me, he seemed to get angry and started to poke me in the chest and said, "You'd better stop working on it and do it because if you don't, you'll get drunk." I'd never seen Frank act this way, and it got my attention (I used to think these old guys went to a special school to learn how to poke you in the chest in rhythm with their speech while they were trying to make a point to a newcomer).

"Made a searching and fearless moral inventory of ourselves."
(Step 4 of Alcoholics Anonymous)

Late the following Saturday night, I started on the fourth step, using the Big Book as my guide. Taking a fourth step is like using a jeweler's loop to examine every nook and cranny of a precious stone, looking for all of its many imperfections. Only when the imperfections are assessed can the stone be chiseled and polished to give it the translucent sheen God originally intended for it. This evaluation is the beginning of a slow and sometimes meticulous process that should continue for a lifetime. Just as there is no perfect stone, there is no perfect human being, and every day is a day to be used to grow and reflect the sunlight of the Spirit better than we did yesterday.

Note: It's impossible for a blade of grass to grow more than a day's growth in a day's time, and so it is with the human condition…

    I didn't think I had any resentments until I actually took the time to put pen to paper late that night. Someone once told me that if you thought of a person and a vernacular came to mind in front of the person's name, chances are you have a resentment against that person. I soon discovered I had a page full of people who fell into that category. I wrote down the causes of my resentment connected with the names on the list and how they affected me personally.
    As I went through my list of fears and started to analyze them for what they really were, I began to see that fears motivated my behavior for most of my life. I remembered a conversation with an old-timer a few months earlier that didn't make sense to me at the time. The man told me that the only known cure for fear was faith, that it's impossible for fear and faith to exist in a person's head at the same time. I started to see that if I were to get rid of the fear in my life, I was going to have to start developing some sort of faith. I always lacked faith in myself and the other people about me. During the five-year period I spent going to other 12-Step meetings, I had absolutely no faith that the process would work for me because I was such a lowlife. And, of course, I had no faith in a Higher Power because I had none at the time. I finally understood that fear is the worst form of self. When I found myself afraid, it was usually because I thought something was going to be taken away from *me*, somebody was going to do something to *me*, or that *I* would not get what *I* felt *I* deserved. It was hard for me to swallow the idea that I was nothing but a scared little boy, despite the facade I tried to present to the outside world.

While examining my sexual conduct over the years, I was in for a rude awakening. I made a short list of the women I had relationships with (in my mind, anything lasting longer than two weeks constituted a relationship). I found it somehow ironic that the six questions related to sexual conduct are found on page 69 of the Big Book.
- Where had we been selfish, dishonest, or inconsiderate?
- Whom had we hurt?
- Did we unjustifiably arouse jealously, suspicion or bitterness?
- Where were we at fault?
- What should have we done instead?
- Was it selfish or not?

A word like "partnership" when it came to relationships was not in my vocabulary. I saw exactly how selfish I was, and it sickened me. I also discovered patterns of behavior I wasn't aware of until they were on paper. Because of my lack of self-esteem, every time I was involved in a long-term relationship, I purchased a vehicle for the woman as a subtle way of buying her affections. Another pattern that I found disheartening, especially when examining my relationship with Kandy, was the fact that every time a woman got too close emotionally, I would start doing little things to annoy her and eventually push her out of my life. Then I'd go and tell the few friends I had about how she left me when I needed her the most.

    I was finished writing my inventory about 3:00 a.m. the following Sunday morning. Although I was sober six and a half months, my mind was still pretty twisted (really?); it had me thinking that I might possibly die in my sleep, and somebody would discover the fourth step paperwork, only to find out what a dirt bag I really was! I immediately got on the phone and called my sponsor. Waking him from a deep sleep, I told Buck that my inventory was finished, and I needed to get together with him ASAP to do my fifth step. Buck groggily told me to meet him at the Seal Beach pier at 5:00 a.m.

"Admitted to God, to ourselves, and another human being the exact nature of our wrongs."
                     (Step 5 of Alcoholics Anonymous)

I was both eager and apprehensive as I arrived at the pier that morning. The sun was just beginning to rise as we sat on the sand discussing my first attempt at taking a look at myself. As I began to read the scribbled list to Buck, he noticed that I didn't have a fourth column in my inventory. On page 65 of the Big Book, an example appears of a common resentment inventory using the following headings:

I'm resentful at:	The cause:	What it affects:

I used this format for my resentment and fear list. Buck stopped me and asked me to read a paragraph in the middle of page 67 of the Big Book. The section suggests that whatever the offending person did had to be taken out of the equation altogether. It also says that the inventory was ours, not the other person's. Buck pointed out a sentence that says, "When we saw our faults, we listed them…" He told me that the black on the page didn't say, "If we saw our faults" or "Maybe we saw our faults." So, in effect, I needed to have a fourth column labeled "My part in it."

He had me grab a pen while he asked some questions. As we examined each of the resentments on the list, Buck would quiz me, telling me to write the answers down on the far right side of the page. By the time we finished this portion of my inventory, there was a fourth column on the sheet! As I gazed at the new column, I saw a lot of things repeated over and over again, as if someone had taken a rubber stamp and gone down the page. I finally understood what my sponsor was talking about concerning the character defects I read about earlier in the Big Book. All six forms of self were scattered throughout the column, along with the "rubber stamp" issues of drinking and drug use.

One of the miracles of the fifth step (although I didn't think so at the time) occurred when Buck told me to look at each name on the list and what I wrote down in the fourth column and ask myself if I owed that person an amends for my behavior, regardless of what they said or did to me. To my shame and dismay, I had to admit that I owed each and every single person on the list an apology of some sort. For the first time in my life, the glare blinding me from seeing my many shortcomings was momentarily removed, and I had an unhindered look at what the problem really was. It was all in my attitudes, perceptions, and reactions that started from between my ears!

When we examined my list of fears, we went through the same question-and-answer exercise to discover areas I needed to improve upon. It became apparent that I needed to develop more faith in myself, the process of the steps, the people trying to help me, and the relationship I was trying to develop with a Power greater than myself. Buck not only helped me identify and analyze the destructive behaviors I too often exhibited with regard to my sexual conduct but other subtle patterns I was guilty of as well.

One of the things that I always admired about my sponsor was that, although he worked with quite a number of other men, he had the unique ability to give someone his undivided attention. During the course of sharing my fifth step, Buck told me things about his own life that had much in common with what I was divulging to him.

It took about three hours to go through everything I'd written down and talk about what I learned about myself so far. When we were done, Buck asked if there was anything I had left out, specifically the deep, dark secrets. He went on to explain that each person coming into the rooms of AA was carrying skeletons in his or her closet—stuff they swore never, ever to share with another human being. The Big Book talks about newcomers who withhold certain facts about their lives, and invariably (invariably means without exception) they got drunk. Buck told me that if I were to "consciously omit" something, it would come back to haunt me. As it turned out, there were one or two items in my closet that I hadn't intended to talk about. I hesitated for a moment and decided to take a leap of faith. I sucked in a deep breath and came clean with everything. I thought Buck would be horrified at what I shared, but he didn't blink an eye. Instead, he stood up, gave me a hug, told me what a good job I'd done, and suggested we get a cup of coffee before the Sunday morning beach meeting.

Taking the fifth step allowed me to catch a glimpse of what and where the problem really was. I discovered that not only was I a full-blown alcoholic, I was also a full-blown liar, cheat, and thief. This also applied to my sober life. About two months earlier, my home group had elected me the tape person. The group recorded all the people that spoke at the Friday night meeting. We needed a new tape recorder with a dubber to make copies, and they gave me the task of purchasing one. I found it necessary to make $150 profit on the acquisition. This was something I later had to admit to the group and pay them back, with interest.

Sunday was my favorite day of the week. First of all, it was my day off from work, unless I had to catch up on a job. Sometimes I would meet my friend Tom early in the morning at the beach to learn how to surf. Buzz had lent me an older, more stable "log" board to get the hang of it. I always looked forward to the gathering later in the morning at Seal Beach, where we would spread a parachute on the sand and have an AA meeting. Afterward, someone would set up volleyball nets, and everyone would hang out and play all afternoon. It was great to chat with friends or just lie out in the sun and listen to the ocean caress the beach. The Sunday morning I completed my fifth step was especially gratifying for me because now there was one person on the planet that finally knew as much about me as I did at the time; I felt like a two-ton burden had been lifted from my shoulders.

The next two weeks found me grinning from ear to ear as I went through all of my daily routines. Several people made comments about how I appeared to be different, but they couldn't put their finger on exactly what had changed. Although I knew I didn't look any different, I felt as if something was beginning to happen on the inside. I did have one sad afternoon, however, when I sold my little hot rod, the Fiat 124 Spider... I'd made the decision a few weeks earlier to part with it in order to pay off some bills. I saw the car again a few days after I sold it, filled with teenagers headed toward the beach, and I smiled, knowing that the new owner appreciated it as much as I did.

I'd recently completed an engine overhaul on a friend's twelve-cylinder Jaguar XJS. He was an attorney who worked at the same law firm as Monica. He brought it back to me late one Thursday afternoon, asking me to perform its thousand-mile service over the weekend. I serviced it Friday and Saturday, addressing a couple of minor bugs. "Jaguar John" drove the car to the Sunday morning beach meeting two weeks after I'd completed my fifth step. I planned to give it its final test drive that afternoon on the way to pick up Sally at the airport. She'd been out of town on business.

The day was much like any other June day in southern California. The sky was a pristine blue, and you could hear the ocean gently lapping on the beach as everyone sat on the parachute enjoying the morning meeting. Afterward, Buck and I had just finished a volleyball game and were sitting on the sand taking a break when he asked me how everything was going. Without hesitation, I looked at my friend and said, "You know, Buck, I've never had it so good." I suddenly realized with amazement that my answer was true in spite of having only someone's bedroom to occupy, a few clothes in a closet, lots of bills to pay, and not much else. My sponsor smiled at me and remarked that maybe there was some hope for me after all...

Later that afternoon, after showering the sand off my body and getting dressed, I took the XJS for its final test drive. Traffic was normal for a sunny Sunday afternoon in southern California. I was in the slow lane doing about seventy miles an hour, so you could imagine how fast everyone else was going. A sudden flash of white was all I saw in front of me before the lights went out. June 24, 1987 proved to be a day that would change my life forever...

Chapter 5
A Journey into the Abyss

I scanned the horizon as Tom and I were getting our wet suits on. I was excited because I knew that today was the day I was going to stand on the long board Buzz had lent me and ride a wave all the way in. The two of us paddled out from the shore in anticipation. Bolsa Chica State Beach had waves that novices and amateurs could catch and ride, looking like pros. We were offshore quite a way out before we turned and pointed our boards toward the beach, waiting for the perfect wave. As it approached, Tom gave me some last-minute pointers. The ocean swelled as Tom yelled to start paddling and got upright on his board. I was able to stand and maneuver the board in concert with the wave. What a feeling of exhilaration! I was finally able to ride a wave all the way in without losing it! I reached the shoreline with a triumphant yell as I walked onto the sand. Tom came in behind me, as excited as I was because he'd been tutoring me for weeks and I was finally able to get it! Tom gazed into my exuberant eyes and sadly said, "Well, dude, you did it and you were great. John, you're one of my best friends, and it breaks my heart to tell you this, but you don't belong here..."

As I slowly opened my eyes, I felt tears trickling into my ears. Gradually, my eyes came into focus. The only things I could see were the ceiling tiles above me. I heard the steady beep and whirring noises of machines on my left side and the whooshing sound of another mechanical-sounding object on the right. *Where am I? What is this place?* These were the thoughts going through my mind as I finally saw a familiar face. My mother's face came into view from the right, and she was looking across from where I was lying, motioning to someone to come to her. My father's form seemed to float in from the left. I opened my mouth to ask what they were doing there, but no sound came out. I was suddenly scared as my mom told me in the simplest of terms that I had been in a car accident, and I was going to be okay. I was unnerved because I couldn't seem to move anything. I remember my eyes darted from side to side, looking at my parents, only to be obstructed by what looked like a thin iron bar on each side of my face.

I never had a recollection of seeing my father cry, and now I was looking at both of my parents, who appeared as if they'd been crying for some time. Their eyes were swollen and red, gazing down at me through their tears with looks that could only be described as showing the unconditional love a parent feels for their child. I'd never experienced a look that seemed to say so much before from another human being. "It's going to be okay, Johnnie," was all I kept hearing as I drifted off again…

As I drifted in and out of consciousness over the next few days, I saw my brother Bob, who was an army nurse stationed in Washington state, my sisters Betty and Linda, as well as Sally. I was told later that Bob was the first of my family to arrive at the hospital and had, in effect, saved my life. He refused to sign a DNR order and spent hours talking into my ear, attempting to bring me back from the dark cavern of unconsciousness I was in. I wasn't told until much later that Sally spent all afternoon and most of the evening waiting for me at John Wayne Airport before taking a taxi home. She didn't know about the accident until the next day, after angrily calling Buzz, wondering why I had stood her up.

The only indication I had about how much time had passed was the morning that Betty and Sally came into my room, announcing that it was July 6, my thirty-first birthday. The doctors said it was okay for me to suck on a Popsicle for a while. Although I felt something in my throat preventing me from talking, I was still able to say "thank you" by mouthing the words. *What kind of mess did I get myself into?* was the question that plagued me as I drifted off again…

The day came when I was awake and coherent enough to communicate with one of my many doctors. In the presence of Betty and Sally, the doctor hesitantly informed me that it was highly unlikely I would ever be able to father a child. He then went on to tell me that I would never walk again and would spend the rest of my life in a wheelchair. (I still find it unfathomable to this day why the doctor felt it was more important to tell me about the chances of fathering a child before he told me that I would never walk again.) I was crushed and soon started slipping into an abyss of depression deeper than I had ever known. As my family and girlfriend came to see me, trying to cheer me up, I could only manage a faint smile, giving everyone a look that was later described to me as one of complete resignation.

After a few weeks with me in the ICU, my mother and father had to fly back to their home in Maine. As they were saying their good-byes, my mother commented on the many friends I had that were praying for me outside in the waiting room. I didn't know it at the time, but my AA friends, including many I didn't know at all, inhabited the waiting room, supporting my parents and family around the clock. I got choked up at the thought of all those unknown people supporting *my* family, just because I was a member of the AA family.

My parents promised they would return at the soonest opportunity. Through my tears I was thinking to myself that I would give anything to be able to hold my parents and tell them how much I loved them. The same thing happened when it came time for my brother and sisters to leave.

Two months after that accident on the southbound side of Interstate 405, I was considered stable enough to be moved out of ICU and into a private room that was considered a step-down unit. This was major progress because I was "coded" ten times during my first thirty days in the hospital. At this point I was allowed visitors other than immediate family. My sponsor and many other friends I didn't even know stopped by for a few minutes each day. They all asked the same question, which annoyed me to no end. They would ask, "What are you grateful for today?" I found myself at times wishing I could get out of the bed and club these people to death because they obviously didn't have a clue what I was going through.

Note: Buck used to ask me on a regular basis to take a slip of paper and write down three or four things I was grateful for that day and put it in my pocket, so that when I got irritated or pissed off at some point, I'd hopefully have the presence of mind to grab it and read it as a reminder. These days, when I'm talking to one of the guys I sponsor and he's complaining about something, I'll stop him in midsentence and say, "Quick! Tell me three things you're grateful for today!"

A respiratory therapist told me the ventilator I was on would probably be necessary for another couple of months. This frustrated me even more because not only was I paralyzed from the chin down, I couldn't verbalize the anger, depression, self-pity, and the other mixed-up, intensely painful emotions that coursed through my mind. I often felt like I was in the middle of an oozing tar pit, being sucked into the darkest regions of oblivion, and the more I tried to escape the more I was drowning in the thick, oily muck of despair. Something happens to a person when he or she is stuck in a dark, seemingly bottomless abyss—whether physical or emotional. The longer you're there, the more of a toll it takes on the human psyche. If one is lucky enough to climb out of and escape its insidious grasp, one finds that something of a paradox occurs; a portion of their soul is lost and gone forever, being replaced by a new, untapped understanding waiting to be explored.

As the days went by at a snail's pace, I was being made aware of how extensive my injuries actually were. My neck was broken in two places that required the fusing and wiring of several vertebrae. After an MRI, it was discovered that my spinal cord was torn completely at the C-7 vertebrae. My left elbow was shattered, and the doctors doubted I would ever be able to straighten my arm again from the ninety-degree angle it was in while in the cast. The doctors explained that a phenomenon occurs when there is trauma to major joints in conjunction with a spinal cord injury. The joint calcifies to the point where it becomes a solid piece of bone, with no soft tissue remaining. My left pelvis was shattered as well from slamming into the door. The catalytic converter of the XJS had somehow been pushed up through the floorboard and had burned my right calf to the bone, requiring skin grafts. Aside from many superficial cuts and bruises, I also had a ruptured spleen, along with massive internal bleeding.

The doctors told me that the good physical shape I was in from all of the running and weight training I'd been doing had contributed to saving my life. *Saving my life for what?* was the only thought that came to mind when I learned this. Strangely enough, the fact that I wasn't wearing a seat belt at the time of the accident also proved to be a factor in saving my life. When the vehicle hit the curb, my upper body slammed into the driver's door and then flopped over to the center of the car. As I was sprawled across the console, the roof caved in from the tumbling motions. If I'd been wearing the shoulder belt, the roof would've stuffed my head down between my shoulders.

Sometime in August, my friend Buck recommended Don, an attorney he knew, to look into the car accident. Don brought a few pictures the Highway Patrol had taken of the XJS shortly after my body was removed from it. It was a barely recognizable twisted hunk of metal. In a brief moment, while gazing at the pictures, I had an epiphany—I went from believing that maybe there is a God to *knowing* there is a God. There was no way I should have made it out of the mangled wreck alive...

As I stared at the photographs of what used to be a car, Don explained what actually transpired that fateful afternoon. While I was driving to the airport, a nineteen-year-old kid who had just tuned up his girlfriend's car raced to change five lanes without signaling and cut me off. I slammed on the brakes to avoid hitting the white Mustang and lost control of the Jaguar. The vehicle went into a power slide, hit the curb sideways, and went airborne, tumbling from side to side and end to end. When the fire department arrived, they put out an engine compartment fire and used the Jaws of Life to peel back the roof to extract my crumpled body. They couldn't find my wallet to identify me but found the registration and assumed I was the owner of the car. As I was being rushed to the Fountain Valley Regional Trauma Center, a few miles away, the Highway Patrol called the car owner's home, finding out that he was actually in the backyard gardening and that I'd been servicing the car over the weekend. The attorney called Monica, and she arrived at the hospital as I was being prepped for surgery. She called Buzz to tell him what happened.

I began to have a vague idea of what my friends were getting at when they would ask me what I was grateful for. The ability to be sucking air, albeit through a machine, was the only thought that came to mind.

Although Don had already made plans to retire, he saw some merit in my case and told me he would stick around long enough to see it through as a favor to Buck. He also told me about his intent to have conversations with the California Bureau of Workmen's Compensation and to investigate highway standards at the California Department of Transportation (DOT) with regard to the placement of the guardrails at the crash site. My mind was a thousand miles away, deep in the dark, endless void of self-pity and anguish, thinking that maybe this all happened to me as a result of some cosmic Karmic Law—to get even with me for all of the rotten things I did to those near and dear to me. I came back to reality long enough to mouth the words "thank you" as Buck and Don left the hospital room, even though I didn't hear a word that was being said at the time.

    I dwelled in the deep chasm of despair that contributed to the demoralizing thoughts going on between my ears. Seeing the pictures of the wreck I was pulled from eventually served as an anchor and lifeline. This helped me to slowly start inching out of the pitch black cavern in my mind. It was a tedious and slow process. One of the recurring questions was *Why me?* and it plagued me constantly amid the beeps and whooshing noises of the machinery still connected to my body, monitoring my condition and keeping me alive...

    In less than three months, my 195-pound muscular frame had wasted away to an emaciated 160 pounds, mostly due to atrophy. The hospital staff started getting me used to being upright in a wheelchair. For the first time, I was able to see what condition I was in when a full-length mirror was placed in front of me. The image in the mirror reflected a withered, gaunt, unkempt form of an unknown man slumped in a chair. The apparition had a metal ring bolted to his head, with rods extending down to what resembled football shoulder pads. The "halo," as it's called, was in place to keep my neck immobile until the surgically repaired vertebrae healed. I was appalled at the figure staring back at me. During the hours I was up in a chair, the respiratory therapist began to ease me off the ventilator. The first time the hose was removed and a plug was inserted in the tube, going down my throat, I couldn't speak above a whisper.

    Every few days, when Buck stopped by to visit, he would take the time to give me a shave in an effort to boost my morale. The huge, meaty hands of a bricklayer would gently guide the razor through the tears that trickled down my cheeks and around the metal bars of the halo contraption bolted directly into my skull. Buck was an example of gentleness and kindness not normally attributed to the male sex. His selfless acts and those of other close friends forced me to realize how totally helpless I actually was. It was against my nature to accept help from anyone. I had pride in the foolish idea that I was self-sufficient and didn't need assistance from anyone... Now the tables were turned on me, and my ego was slowly being pulverized into nothingness, regardless of how hard I resisted. This crushing process soon began to manifest itself in a constant despondency that began to worry those close to me. Thoughts of just "checking out" began to dominate the gloomy recesses of my mind...

My arrogance and refusal to ask for help when I needed it, in spite of my present circumstance, came to the forefront one day while alone in my room. I was lying in bed, gazing at the ceiling, when somehow a fly appeared out of nowhere. It kept circling my head and landing on my nose. At that time I couldn't move anything from my chin down, so I wasn't able to swat it away. All I could do was wiggle my nose and blow at the fly through my mouth. This went on for what seemed like hours. The fly reduced me to tears before I managed to blow into the tube, calling a nurse to kill it. Can you imagine a grown man crying because of a little fly?

Every person on this planet, regardless of his or her station in life, takes so much for granted, until something catastrophic happens to upset the equilibrium. Any life-changing cataclysm will eventually force a person to examine the facets of his or her personal "life stone" from a different angle and reorganize priorities if they are to survive free of the multitude of negative and caustic attitudes sure to come to the forefront. My self-esteem was lower than it ever had been; I kept thinking about the daily mundane tasks of showering, shaving, brushing my teeth, going to the bathroom, and even breathing on my own—everyday jobs that I never gave a second thought to. I was forced to think about a life completely dependent on the kindness and charity of others—if I was going to decide to live at all.

Challenging situations can either bring out the best in the human spirit or the worst, depending upon the awareness and experiences a person has had up to the point of adversity. Each person, whether he or she admits it or not, has seen "red flags" go up in their mind's eye regarding human relationships, romantic or otherwise. I started seeing "red flags" in my relationship with Sally, dismissing them because I was using my own unreliable scale of judgment to look at what might be a problem down the road.

The first indication that something was wrong came up during a conversation with Buck. He hesitantly told me about an argument Sally started with him concerning the attorney he found to look into my accident, stating that Don was "too inept to handle a case of this magnitude." I also later learned that shortly after the accident Monica and Sally met in the ICU waiting room. What started as a discussion about my condition soon escalated into name-calling and shrieking outbursts from both women. Sally had Monica barred from the hospital on the grounds that she was no longer relevant in my life (I later rectified that when I made amends to Monica).

The hair on the back of my neck rose one afternoon when Buzz and his wife Janet stopped by to visit. Not only was Buzz my employer, but he and I had also been close friends for years. We skied together, drank together the night Janet gave birth to their first son, confided in each other, and even got into harmless mischief together. Buzz never fully understood my reasons for going to treatment and getting sober, but he always respected me for it. As we relived old escapades, I was laughing for the first time in months. Sally entered the hospital room. Upon seeing Buzz, she went into a tirade. She accused Buzz of being involved in a sort of conspiracy with the California Department of Workman's Compensation to deny the money she thought I deserved because I was working on a customer's car at the time of the accident. The room went silent as Buzz gave me a wounded stare and then a quizzical look that seemed to ask, "What is this woman's problem? Do you believe that I'd do something like that to you?"

My face burned with embarrassment as Buzz and Janet mumbled their good-byes. I could only glare at Sally, seething with anger because I didn't have the words at that moment to articulate the hurt, humiliation, and absolute rage I felt because of her rudeness to my friends.

I had a fleeting moment of pride when Buzz called a week later, informing me that the "infamous" Jaguar XJS I repaired after coming out of treatment was once again inhabiting the shop—this time the water pump had gone bad. Buzz had never done the repair on that model before and was asking me for help. I was able to tell him how to do it efficiently (using a couple of trade secrets) and repair it once and for all. Buzz told me that the customer was somehow convinced I put thousands of miles on his car going to Las Vegas and points in between. I assured him that wasn't the case.

Note: This was one of the few times in my life when I was being accused of doing something that I didn't do!

The team of doctors, nurses, and social workers spent the last two weeks of September talking about the improvements I'd made and the necessity of moving on. I was given three options: rehab at the Rancho Los Amigos Rehabilitation Center in Downey; going to rehab at St. Jude's Hospital in Fullerton; or the least attractive alternative, going to a nursing home. I somehow assumed if I were going to a nursing home, it would be to wait and eventually die…

Sometime during the month, I made the difficult and fundamental decision to live, so the nursing home option was out of the question. I didn't realize it at the time, but the hardest choice of my life would come months later.

Note: It's a good thing that we live our lives twenty-four hours at a time. If I'd known what was in store for me when I first got sober, I would have cut and run.

Not knowing what the physical rehabilitation process required, I used the location of the facilities to influence the choice I was going to make. St. Jude's Hospital was in Orange County, where I had lived and worked before the accident, so it was a no-brainer as far as I was concerned. October 1 was scheduled to be the day I would take the next step in the rehabilitation process of my body and mind.

That morning turned out to be quite a memorable one as I mentally prepared for the transfer to St. Jude's Hospital. I was in a Clinitron bed that weighed almost a thousand pounds, circulating air to make the tiny sand-like pieces gently move around its sealed enclosure. That morning the Whittier Narrows Earthquake hit, and although it was only a magnitude 5.9 quake, my bed started bouncing across the second-floor hospital room like a tennis ball toward the window. As the bed neared the window, my only thought was, *Well, I guess I'm going to be the new parking lot attendant.* This tiny bit of humor showed that my attitude was starting to make minute changes…

The ambulance ride to St. Jude's Hospital was interrupted later that afternoon when we had to pull over a couple of times because of a few of the aftershocks. Once the ambulance arrived, having carefully made the trip on side streets that had no traffic lights, I was rolled on a gurney to my new room. I was put onto the same kind of bed I had at the Fountain Valley hospital when a team of nurses came in to evaluate my condition.

The team was headed by an older nurse, Joan, who obviously was close to retirement. She seemed to draw a certain respect from the staff, even though she was so crotchety in the way she told her fellow nurses in her thick New England accent to turn me as they poked and prodded. They discovered a number of decubitus ulcers (pressure sores) on my buttocks from the hours I spent upright in a chair without proper cushioning. Joan remarked that although the Trauma Center had done an excellent job of saving my life, they scored a "zero" in her book because of the condition of my rump. I remember asking her for a pain shot, and she answered, "Sure thing, sonny, where do you want it?" I told her that I didn't care as long as I couldn't feel it (I have no feeling below my chest).

The sight of the large woman coming at me with a needle that seemed six inches long made me a little nervous. Joan stuck the needle in my shoulder, causing me to wince. I thought to myself, *Oh great, is this what I'm in for?* as I drifted off.

Chapter 6
Life-Changing Decisions

The first few days at St. Jude's Hospital were spent being examined by doctors and nurses in their effort to evaluate the condition I was in and to form a plan of action. Even though I was despondent and really didn't care about what was going on around me, I followed their suggestions and soon started a routine of going to both physical and occupational therapies scheduled by the staff.

Don hired a crew to follow me around and film a typical day at the hospital for use as evidence in court, should it get to that point. Mornings would start with me being fed breakfast because I didn't have the ability to do it for myself. Then would start the two to three hour "getting ready for the day" process of being physically transferred onto a shower/commode chair and rolled down the hall to the bathroom, where my nurse would give me a suppository to enable a bowel movement, and subsequently she would give me a shower. Then there was the transfer back to my bed so that the dressings on my many wounds could be changed, and the nurse would clothe me. I had to wear a girdle called an "abdominal binder" around my stomach in order to keep my organs in place and to help keep my blood pressure close to normal.

The final transfer of the morning would be to a rickety electric wheelchair (it was actually an old chrome-plated manual hospital wheelchair that had been retrofitted with a small electric motor rubbing against the rear tires) that I could drive on my own once my upper limbs were placed in the troughs built into each armrest. The fact that I could now move my wrists allowed me to manipulate the joystick and direct the wheelchair down the hall to the elevator. I'd have to wait for someone to come by and press the button to call the elevator as well as the inside button to the basement for the first physical therapy session of the day.

It was really quite an undertaking for Tricia, the physical therapist assigned to work with me, to transfer me from the wheelchair to a mat that was on a platform about one and a half feet off the ground. Not only was I essentially dead weight because of the paralysis, but I was also encumbered by the shoulder pads and the iron monstrosity bolted to my skull, making me top-heavy. She would manage the transfer onto the mat, get me flat on my back, and stretch the atrophied muscles in my legs to the point that I sometimes thought she would break a bone. She attempted to teach me how to roll my lifeless body on the mat using leverage. Having my left arm frozen in a ninety-degree position made it extremely difficult. It was also hard for me to maintain any balance without assistance while sitting on the edge of the mat. I'd spend time with two-pound ankle weights strapped to the palms of my hands, trying to strengthen my withered wrists. We endured this monotonous routine twice a day, Monday through Friday, with only Trisha contributing to the conversation because my mind was elsewhere.

The second part of the morning would be spent with the occupational therapist. I found I was able to flex my wrists a bit shortly before relocating to the rehab hospital. The therapist taught me a technique called tenodesis to use my paralyzed hands to pick up small objects. When I flexed my wrist toward the inside of the forearm, my fingers would naturally extend. As I drew my wrist backward, the tendons in my fingers would cause them to close in on whatever object I was trying to pick up. It seemed as if eons were spent on stacking cardboard cones and moving rubber balls, but I soon started to get the hang of it. She also tried to teach me how to eat unassisted by first fixing a counterbalance contraption on to the corner of the wheelchair and placing my arm in it. The morning that the crew was filming, I was attempting to eat Jell-O for the first time with a spoon strapped to my hand. I was able to get about one-third of it into my mouth, while the rest ended up on my face or dropped onto the table.

I'm left-handed, and it was tough learning how to write again with the adaptive device the therapist suggested. Since my left arm was now solid at a right angle, I had to use my entire shoulder to manipulate the pen across the page. I often thought to myself that my writing was much more legible when I was a first-grader.

There was a common area where all of the patients congregated for lunch. Although people had been feeding me for months, I still found it humiliating to rely on someone for such a simple task. After lunch, I would track down my nurse for the day and go to my room, where she would catheterize me in order to void the urine in my bladder. I learned to pay special attention to my fluid intake between catheterizations, or I would end up wetting myself like an infant. It never failed that when the nurse pulled down my sweatpants to sterilize my penis before inserting the catheter, she would somehow get Betadine solution all over the sweats, staining them, which embarrassed and frustrated me all the more.

After lunch and the catheterization fiasco in my hospital room, I would take a half hour or so to myself and sit in the sun on the patio outside of the lunchroom. I'd close my eyes and feel the warm rays of the sun baking the parts of my useless body I could feel, while I mentally tried to escape my pathetic situation, if even for only a few moments. Sometimes the sunshine would be so intense that the metal of the halo would heat up to the point where I could feel the bolts almost burning holes into my head. I often found myself wishing that the hot bolts would somehow cook the memories, good and bad, out of my consciousness.

One morning, while I was enduring the process of getting ready for the day, a nurse turned me on my side and I felt something strange happen in my temples where the bolts were located for the halo device. I didn't know it at the time, but the bolts holding my head securely in the halo were supposed to be retightened from time to time. Not doing so was an oversight by the staff, and as a result, when I was turned over onto my side, my head literally came out of the halo. A doctor was immediately called. When he arrived, a team of nurses gently rolled me onto my back.

The doctor told me that they needed to relocate the bolts on the halo to a different location while assuring me that a local anesthetic would alleviate any discomfort I might feel. I felt a little uncomfortable at the thought of new bolts being attached to my skull while still awake but agreed to the procedure. The local was administered and the doctor began to reinstall the bolts. The pain was incredible. One of the nurses told me later that she heard my shrieks while she was in the elevator down the hall.

The afternoon schedule was a repeat of the morning's therapy routine ending about 3:30 p.m. Although patients required a pass to go to different areas of the hospital, I would venture into the secluded little chapel on the first floor or wander outside to the garden area next to the main building in an attempt to find a quiet moment of respite from the voices of self-pity, the "what ifs," and "why me's" somehow still constantly plaguing me. The day would end with dinner that was usually served at 5:30 p.m.

I always looked forward to Wednesday evenings because a few guys from my home group would meet on the patio, and we'd have an AA meeting. It gave me a chance to talk with Jerry M., Alan R., Bob S., Mike M., and, of course, my sponsor. It was also an opportunity to connect with the world outside of the hospital environment. During the course of the meeting, I would invariably vent my frustrations and anxieties about what I perceived to be a future miserable existence. I was having a tough time visualizing life beyond the hospital, totally helpless now that I was a quadriplegic. My friends would patiently listen to my sniveling, eventually asking me why I wasn't more grateful than just to be sucking air, but the question fell on deaf ears…

I wasn't the only one complaining about their situation. Sally would visit me at least once a week (without ever offering to participate in the rehab process I was undergoing) and would call every night. I found myself sullenly listening to her go on about how God was doing this (me being in a wheelchair) to her, how she was having a rough time of it at work, and how being a single mom without the support of her boyfriend was too much for her to bear. The red flags were waving in my face again at this point, but I didn't act on the warning.

November 2, 1987, was my first sober anniversary. It was customary at AA meetings to celebrate someone's anniversary as if it were his or her birthday (for most people it was as if they were actually reborn). I was told about a large weekly meeting held in the basement of the hospital. Buck suggested that we go to the meeting together to celebrate the occasion. I had a concern that I couldn't "take a cake" because of all the drugs I was being given. He smiled in his usual way and asked, "John, did you get into your accident so that you could get high?" He reminded me that the drugs were being administered by medical personnel for a medical purpose, and that I didn't need to worry about it. As we were going down the elevator to the basement, Buck told me that this particular meeting didn't celebrate birthdays until the end of the month, but it would be good for me to go to this meeting anyway. The meeting was held in the staff cafeteria, and as we entered the double doors, I was shocked to see that almost everyone from my Friday night home group was there!

The meeting had taken a vote and made an exception at the request of my home group members to celebrate my first sober anniversary that evening. I barely had enough strength to blow out the lone candle on the cake as everyone sang "Happy Birthday." The expansive room got so quiet that you could hear a pin drop as everyone waited for me to say something. Through a stream of tears, I managed to thank everyone for making it such a special evening. I remember talking about how I was told that things would get better if I stayed sober and took the steps. I frankly admitted that things got different and not necessarily better, and that for today, I was okay with that. The rest of the meeting was a blur as I tried to deal with all of the emotions welling up inside. After the meeting, I mingled for what seemed like hours with my friends who had taken the trouble to come out that evening to see me. Later that night, when a nurse helped me into bed, I felt as if I'd just run a marathon.

Tricia was getting increasingly frustrated with me—she did *all* the work every day, and although I was there physically, I wasn't mentally or emotionally present. The morning after the late night with my friends, I didn't feel like getting up, so I decided to stay in bed. Tricia came into my room with an angry look that totally surprised me. She said, "I've had enough of your lousy attitude and you feeling sorry for yourself. There are people here who are a lot worse off than you are, and they're trying to improve. It seems like you don't care about anything or anyone but yourself. This is the way it's going to be—if you don't want to be bothered about making your life better with what you have left, I won't either. I cannot and will not help a guy who won't help himself. I've seen and been with enough losers in my life to know that they're hopeless. John, you've gotten some return back, and it's not unreasonable to think that you could get even more back if you were to work at it. Since you're here in bed for the rest of the day, I want you to think about this; you have a choice to make—either show up at therapy tomorrow prepared to do some work, or stay in your bed and wallow in self-pity and eventually die—I don't care. If you do decide to show up tomorrow, I'll do everything I can to help you. If you don't, I'm not going to waste my time with you."

I'd never seen Tricia this emotional. She was so mad that she was in tears. She turned and left the room, leaving me with a life-changing choice. What was I going to do?

For the rest of the day and late into the night, I thought seriously about what Tricia said, especially the references she made to me being a loser. I'd been called that many times in my life, and for the second time it really bothered me. It's one thing to make the basic decision to live or die; it's quite another to make your mind up to really live your life or just exist. My thoughts went way back to the days before I got sober, and I remembered always having the vague feeling that I was taking up someone else's space or that I was sucking someone else's air because I didn't belong here on Earth. Could it be that God had some reason for sparing my life? Was there some Divine purpose at work here? How was I going to be of any use to anyone or anything while stuck in a wheelchair? These were the kind of questions that were intertwined with recollections of events that seemed to happen a lifetime ago as I finally drifted off to sleep.

The next morning, it was as if I were a different person. I was eager to get through breakfast, as well as the usual morning routine. I made the trip down the elevator to the therapy unit, greeting Tricia with a smile and saying, "Let's get busy." She suggested that we start improvising with what was available. As I was lying flat on the mat, I asked to have a twenty-pound weight put on my diaphragm to help strengthen my breathing. With a look of amazement, Tricia added more weight when I told her that it wasn't enough to make me really work at it. The unit had a multitude of different-sized ankle weights, and we experimented with them to develop strength and range of motion in my upper body because I was now able to move my arms. As the weeks went by, Tricia and I developed a specialized exercise routine adapting other pieces of equipment for our needs.

Even the occupational therapist found it odd that I was smiling while stacking cones and asking lots of questions about the different adaptive devices I'd like to try. In no time, with the help of some of these strap-on cuffs, I was getting stronger and within a few weeks was finally able to feed myself without the counterbalance mechanism, as well as a nurse hovering over me waiting for a mishap. I was fully participating in my physical and emotional recovery but still had a long way to go...

A huge step forward was the day I was given an older Invacare electric wheelchair to use instead of the "chrome rat trap" that was breaking down all the time. As I was spending more time in my chair, the head nurse of the ward started to show me things I should do to avoid skin breakdowns on my butt. We found the best match for me was a Roho cushion that had individual air cells that could be inflated to match my body's contours. I was told that if I used this kind of cushioning in conjunction with regularly shifting my weight, the skin on my bottom would be just fine.

One morning, Don came to see me with the news of a settlement offer from the California Bureau of Workmen's Compensation. They suggested that although a portion of what I was doing was actually work-related and because of my present physical state, I would probably only live three years, and it justified a one-time settlement offer of over $700,000 to be used at my discretion. I questioned Don about the source of the statistical data they were using in regard to my life expectancy but agreed with him that the offer should be taken seriously. I approved the settlement and told Don to take his fee off the top and bring me a check for the balance. A week later, he brought me a check for just under $660,000 and reminded me that we still had an ongoing case with the California DOT, so it wasn't over yet. I got permission from the powers that be to roll across the street to the nearest bank with Buck and open an account. I deposited $600,000 into a CD and the rest into a checking account.

With my newfound financial assets, I was finally able to address the bills that had been piling up and the collection agencies that were trying to contact me. I paid all of the credit cards off and closed the accounts. I also paid Buzz the money I still owed him and a little extra for the money he'd lost because of the jobs that were ongoing at the time of the accident. The collection agency that seemed most difficult to deal with was the one in connection with my hospital stay for substance abuse treatment. I learned, through a series of phone calls, that my medical insurance had dropped me because they felt I lied on the original application for coverage. One of the questions on the application was "Have you ever had a problem with alcohol or drugs?" At the time I was still in denial and honestly felt I didn't have a problem. Upon review of my medical records after treatment, the insurance company came to the conclusion that I was lying all along and refused to pay the bill. So I was left on my own with an $18,000 bill to pay. After several lengthy phone calls with hospital billing department, I was finally able to negotiate a deal and paid $6,000 to square up with the treatment center that saved my life.

While discovering new ways of dealing with my situation and aggressively pursuing the rehab process, I found myself becoming increasingly frustrated that the nightly conversations I was having with Sally centered around her world. The waving red flags now became signal flares. The only thing she talked about was how miserable her life was. I finally came to the conclusion that if I was going to focus on rehab without any distractions, this relationship was going to have to end. I tried to bring the subject up subtly at first but couldn't get through to her.

Things finally came to a head a few days before Christmas of 1987, when Sally came to visit. She brought me a bathrobe as a present, and it was the final straw. I pointed out to her that in my present state, it was useless to me—what was she thinking? I also remarked about how aggravated I was with her constant complaining and how she couldn't or wouldn't "get out of herself" long enough to see what I was going through. I went on to tell her that I didn't appreciate the comments she made to Buck about his choice of attorneys—that it wasn't really any of her business anyway. When I brought up the embarrassment she'd caused me in front of Buzz and Janet, my face felt flushed and the hair went up on the back of my neck. The more I talked, the angrier I got. I finally told her to leave the hospital and my life and never come back.

It was a major deal for me a few days later when the cumbersome metal halo was finally removed. My neck was extremely weak from lack of use, so it required that I wear a foam neck brace until the muscles necessary to hold my head upright without fatigue were strong enough. I found a new obstacle to surmount in physical therapy and approached it with enthusiasm.

The highlight of the holiday was Pee-Wee's visit with his bride, Monique. I met her when visiting Maine before the car accident. I had no idea that they were engaged to be married. We had fun talking and catching up on everything. They accompanied me to therapy sessions throughout the day and met the staff who played such an important part of my rehabilitation. I was concerned that my brother was spending too much time in the hospital with me and wasn't devoting enough attention to his new wife. One afternoon, I pulled him aside and asked him to please take her to Disneyland to play tourist for a day. It was a bittersweet afternoon when I said good-bye to the happy couple as they left to fly home.

My pals at the Wednesday night meeting started to notice subtle changes in my attitude. Instead of complaining most of the time, I was talking about the progress I was making and how much stronger I felt. They later told me that they all talked among themselves about how I'd finally turned the corner and was coming back from a place in my mind that they couldn't even imagine. During a conversation with my occupational therapist, I found out that if I managed to get strong enough and develop enough range of motion, I might be able to drive again. I was excited at the thought of having so much freedom; to be able to come and go as I pleased. At one of the Wednesday night gatherings, the general consensus was voiced that it was time for me to get back into the twelve steps…

"Were entirely ready to have God remove all these defects of character."
(Step 6 of Alcoholics Anonymous)

After completing the fifth step with Buck on the beach that seemed so long ago, I was so elated at having done it that I didn't take the time to look at the following step, just like a lot of people do. It's suggested in the Big Book that the sixth step be done immediately after the fifth, and it's the only step that says to take a pause (an hour) and carefully review what's been done up until that point. As it turned out for me, the pause was several months long...

Late one night, while awake in my hospital bed, I went back and thought about how I worked the first five steps. I felt satisfied that I did the very best I could at the time and hadn't cut any corners. I learned a lot about myself and discovered certain defects of character in my makeup that had to be eliminated. I was willing to do something about it. There were also areas in my life that needed to drastically improve, or I'd be forever miserable. Tricia's earlier angry tirade helped to give me the kick in the pants I needed to get restarted. The two paragraphs in the Big Book that describe the sixth step emphasize willingness as being a major part of the process. I once again found myself willing to do anything, as only the dying can be. The question came to mind: *Now what am I going to do about it?*

"Humbly asked Him to remove our shortcomings."
(Step 7 of Alcoholics Anonymous)

I opened my Big Book to page 76 and saw that the seventh step is only one paragraph long, and it was in the form of a prayer. I also noticed something different from the third-step prayer I'd already learned; the word "Amen" was at the end of this prayer. *"My Creator, I am now willing that you should have all of me, good and bad. I pray that you now remove from me every single defect of character which stands in the way of my usefulness to you and my fellows. Grant me strength, as I go out from here, to do your bidding. Amen."*

Sometime later, an old-timer friend named Don M. pointed out to me that the word "Amen" didn't appear at the end of the third-step prayer because it was a subtle indication that work needed to be done between steps three and seven, and once that was accomplished, the two prayers became one. Upon learning this little-known fact, I began my mornings with the third and seventh step prayers, and things started ever so slowly to change in my perceptions and the way I reacted to the world around me.

Throughout the months of January and February 1988, it felt as if I was on a mission. I attacked every workout in physical therapy, collaborating with Tricia, always trying a new exercise or movement with the limited equipment at hand. I'd developed friendships with many of the staff, especially the crotchety head nurse, Joan. I was amazed to discover that as soon as *my* attitude started to change, the staff seemed to come out of the woodwork, offering tips that would come in handy for me down the road. As I became more confident, I started to stretch the envelope. Not being one to follow the rules too well, and even though a pass was needed to go to specific areas of the hospital, I often went without one while exploring every corner of the hospital and its grounds. There were even a few sunny afternoons when I "escaped" and rolled down the street to have lunch at a restaurant (hospital food was getting old) and returned before anybody knew I was gone.

In early March, I received a telephone call that was totally unexpected: Monique called to tell me that Pee-Wee was in Boston General Hospital and was dying of cancer. I knew that he had a bout with cancer a few years earlier, and everyone thought it was in remission. I tried everything I could to get out of St. Jude's and fly to Boston to be with my brother, but I wasn't far enough along in my rehab to do it. After exhausting all possibilities, I called him on a Wednesday afternoon for what was going to be the last time. When Pee-Wee answered the phone, I could tell he was really weak and seemed to be disoriented because of the painkillers he was on. My other brother Bob was there, holding the phone next to Pee-Wee's ear as he seemed to babble on. After a while, I finally told him to shut up and that I had something really important to tell him.

I knew deep in my heart that I was never going to see him again and that I should use this opportunity to make amends for the things that I'd done. I admitted all of the stuff that I could remember having done to my youngest brother while we were growing up and the lies I was guilty of when we became adults. It seemed like I talked forever, and when I was finished, I asked Pee-Wee a question: "Is there anything else I've ever done to cause you harm or embarrassment that I am not aware of?"

And then a miracle happened. Pee-Wee's voice came through the telephone line clearly and concisely as he told me, "John you don't have anything to be sorry for. If anything, you've been an inspiration for me." I wasn't ready for a response like that. The idea that I could be an inspiration to anyone was amazing to me because I'd spent so much time wallowing in self-pity, never thinking that someone was watching me. As I said good-bye to Pee-Wee, I choked back the tears because of what he had said, and I *knew* we'd never speak again.

I hung up the phone, stunned by my brother's response, and through the tears streaming down my face I found my thoughts drifting back to the very first meeting of Alcoholics Anonymous I attended while I was still in treatment. The speaker that night (Bill H.) gave his talk while sitting in a wheelchair.

Note: I made a conscious decision then and there that if I could carry even a fraction of the message that Bill carried to me at that Friday night meeting, I would make it my life's purpose from that point on.

Pee-Wee passed away three days later...

Chapter 7
Necessity is the Mother of Invention

It was a few days shy of Pee-Wee's twenty-fourth birthday when I received the phone call from my sister Linda about his death. Buck arrived at the hospital shortly afterward to console me. It eased my pain just a bit when he reminded me of the fact that I no longer had any "shoulda, woulda, couldas" when it came to my relationship with Pee-Wee. The weekend seemed to last forever because I didn't have anything to do but think about my brother and about how his bride Monique must be feeling at the loss of her husband.

Monday finally arrived, and I went to the morning physical therapy session, telling Tricia of the news I received over the weekend. I worked harder than ever that day, as if I could somehow vent the pain, frustration, and anger I felt as I tried to take it all out on the weights and equipment.

Although my family understood why I couldn't attend the funeral, I still felt guilty for not being there. My parents told me that Pee-Wee would want me to concentrate on rehabilitation so that I could get out of the hospital and develop some normalcy in my life. I thought about the word "normalcy" and how it could ever apply to me, but I promised to do the best I could.

The team overseeing my care told me in mid-March that it was time to start thinking about where I was going to go after my rehab was over. An occupational therapist came to see me one afternoon to measure me for a new electric wheelchair, a manual chair, and shower chair that I'd need once I left St. Jude's. She told me that the Quickie manual and shower chairs would arrive in a few weeks because they were standard items when considering my body measurements. The electric wheelchair, however, was going to take some time because it would have to be custom-built, so they would lend me the power chair I was using at the time until the new one was finished.

It was imperative that if I were to spend time up in a chair, I'd have to shift my body weight from time to time to prevent pressure sores from developing on my bottom. There were several systems available that would lay out flat and stretch a person completely prone while in his or her chair, or one system that would enable the user to tilt back forty-five degrees while keeping the same sitting position. I opted for the tilt-back system because my mechanical background told me that going from a sitting position to a prone position would have a tendency to drag my butt across whatever cushion I was using, increasing the possibility of a skin tear or breakdown.

Buck started to attend physical therapy with me two or three afternoons a week so that Tricia could teach him how to transfer me from a wheelchair to his car. During the first few attempts, my head bounced off the roofline of my sponsor's Datsun 260Z, causing us all to laugh. It didn't take long, however, for Buck and I to get the hang of it without denting his car or my head.

Almost everyone in the rehab unit felt that I should consider going to a halfway house for the disabled in order to make the transition to independent living. I readily agreed to explore the idea, since the only other option available was a nursing home. It was this motivation that prepared me for the next phase of recovery…

I was told about a transitional living center in Paramount, California, and agreed to go on a site visit. The place was called Winners, and it was a modest three-bedroom ranch home that catered only to quadriplegics and paraplegics striving to achieve independent living. Everything in the plain-looking home had been remodeled for easy wheelchair access. Each bedroom had two hospital beds, two small dressers, and an open closet space. In the kitchen, the cabinets were lowered and the countertops were open underneath to facilitate wheelchair use. The garage behind the house was set up as a recreational and exercise area with a universal gym modified for use in a sitting position. The neighborhood was in a rough part of town that was predominantly Hispanic. Although I wasn't thrilled at the idea of living in L.A. County, I filled out an application and was told that a bed would be available sometime in mid to late April.

While I was waiting for an opening at Winners, I wanted to make the best of the time I had left at St. Jude's. One of my major concerns was having to rely on someone to catheterize me periodically throughout the day. There had to be some way around it if I wanted to be as independent as possible. I talked with a urologist on staff at the hospital, who suggested that I get a "super pubic" catheter as soon as possible. The doctor explained that a minor surgery was needed to allow the catheter direct access to my bladder, and it would only have to be replaced once a month. The catheter would drain constantly into a concealed leg bag attached to it, and I could empty it every so often on my own. While waiting for the surgery, I checked out different leg bags as well as optional drain valve setups.

After the procedure was performed at the end of March, I discovered that the sweatpants I wore wouldn't work because of the elastic cuff at the bottom of the pants. It prevented access to the drain valve located next to my ankle. I was going to have to get some "regular" clothes if this was going to work. Through trial and error methods requiring lots of patience, I finally found pants that would do the job. I had to take into consideration the fact that my body's dimensions had changed so much. After getting the first pair of new pants, I got busy teaching myself to drain the leg bag efficiently without outside help.

The last few weeks at St. Jude's Hospital were emotional because of the close bonds I had with the people that went out of their way to work with me. It was especially difficult to express the gratitude I felt for Tricia, who'd become such a close friend. The day she came into my hospital room and chewed me out was not only *the* turning point in my rehabilitation, but it also aided in my decision to live life to the fullest, ultimately affecting my overall attitude.

As I reflected over the ten months I spent hospitalized, I came to the realization that I owed everyone who had so patiently worked with me an amends for my behavior. So in the last few weeks I was at St. Jude's, I sought out every staff member that I was rude to and had treated so poorly. I told them all that I was wrong and out of line in the things I said and did. I asked them what I could do to make things right. Almost everyone told me that an apology wasn't necessary because they saw it every day as part of their job, and either their patients changed or they didn't and would end up suffering the consequences of having a miserable life.

Note: Things always work out one of two ways—either they do or they don't...

Tricia was the hardest for me to approach. Through many tears, I was able to convey to her how bad I felt about the way I treated her early on in our relationship and thanked her for setting me straight the way she did. She told me how proud she was of me, and the only thing she wanted for me was to continue on the road of rehabilitation and maybe come back and visit them after my discharge from the hospital.

"Made a list of people we had harmed and became willing to make amends to them all."
(Step 8 of Alcoholics Anonymous)

Something was happening to me during these early experiences at making amends. Although it was painful and emotional for me to admit my wrongs, the flip side was an unexpected sense of freedom. After relating this to a few of my friends, I took Buck's advice to "read the black on the page," specifically when it came to eighth step. I started with a steno pad and wrote a list of names of people with whom I had resentments from my fourth step inventory (regardless of what they had done, I *knew* I owed them an amends for *my* part in things). I then went back through my life and thought of all the people to whom I'd caused harm or embarrassment to and added them to the list. What started out as a small collection of names suddenly became a book. Buck told me that once my list was completed, three columns should be placed next to the names. The first column would be labeled "ASAP"—in other words—as soon as possible. If I was willing to make amends to that person right now, a checkmark could be put in the column. The second column was to be labeled "maybe." If it applied to a person on the list, the checkmark would go into that column. Then, of course, there was the infamous "never" column. I had several names on the list I'd never be able to or wasn't willing enough to make amends to. Buck told me not to worry about the "maybe" or the "never" columns because all we were going to concentrate on were the names that fell into the ASAP column.

NAME	ASAP	MAYBE	NEVER

The day finally came in mid-April when I made the move to Winners. That morning, there were many tearful good-byes with the doctors, nurses, and therapists who had been so kind and patient with me in spite of my at times disrespectful attitude. As I boarded the van, an immense sense of gratitude to the people who helped me and a feeling of relief came over me as this chapter was closing and a new one was beginning...

My first afternoon at the ranch home in Paramount was spent being introduced to the staff and the residents. One of the two attendants picked to help me—one for days, the other for the night shift—and I organized my few possessions in the new room. Both the shower and the manual wheelchairs ordered a few weeks earlier had been shipped directly to Winners and were already there by the time I arrived. That evening at dinner, I devoured the first home-cooked meal I'd had in over ten months.

Later, I talked to the late shift attendant about the fact that even though I'd be sleeping in a hospital bed, it had a regular mattress on it. She explained to me that this required turning me from side to side every two hours during the night to prevent skin breakdowns.

When it was time to turn in, I was in my bedroom glancing around for a mechanical lift resembling the ones that were used while I was hospitalized. Rosa came in and told me to pull up alongside the bed and trust her. She asked me to turn off my chair and lean over a little so she could remove my shirt and abdominal binder. She then helped me to sit upright again and removed the foot pedals, as well as my shoes. While standing in front of me, she pinched my knees between hers and bent forward slightly, asking me to drape my arms over her shoulders and give her a hug. As soon as I did, Rosa wrapped her arms around the small of my back, stood up enough to get my weight off the wheelchair, and swung me gently over onto the bed. After laying me flat and seeing the surprised look on my face, she told me the "quad pivot" that we'd just done was much quicker and easier than having to maneuver a bulky lift around the small bedroom. She assured me that provided she used the correct body mechanics, there was no strain on her. Rosa finished undressing me and connected my catheter to a special urine collection bag hung on the frame of the bed. Even though I was turned every two hours that first night, I still slept like a rock...

The next morning I was extremely anxious to explore the neighborhood and discovered that the sidewalks and pedestrian crossings were not even close to being as smooth as the hospital floors I'd gotten so used to. As I crossed the first intersection, I encountered a situation that I couldn't have ever anticipated. My wheelchair hit a crack in the asphalt, jarring me and causing both of my legs to spasm. I must have been quite a sight crossing the street with both legs off the foot pedals and flopping straight out in front of me. I was thankful for the chair's seatbelt, or I'd have slid right out onto the street. Once I made it to the other side of the street, it took a few moments for my legs to relax enough so that I could place them back onto the foot pedals. I looked around for a bit and finally saw a hardware store in a strip mall down the street. I slowly and carefully went there to buy a roll of two-inch-wide sticky-backed Velcro and asked the clerk if he would help me cut strips of the material and attach them to the foot pedals as well as to the bottoms of my shoes. Afterward, I tested the new modification by racing across the same intersection at full speed, finding that my feet stayed in place without a single spasm. Later that afternoon, Joyce, the day shift attendant assigned to help me, was able to attach strips of Velcro to the bottoms of all my shoes. I came to the conclusion that necessity really is the mother of invention.

Upon my discharge from St. Jude's, the doctors prescribed Darvocette to help counteract the phantom pains I experienced every day. (Imagine for a moment, if you will, lying in one position for a period of time and having your legs fall asleep. The prickly pins and needles sensation that you get after moving the limbs that "fell asleep" is what I experience on a daily basis—24/7, without exception.) The medication only made me feel groggy and wasn't doing what it was supposed to anyway, so after a few days, I flushed the pills and decided to manage the lingering nonexistent pain on my own. I started a regime of stretching my hamstring muscles to lessen the spasms, as well as the pain I endured, and it worked!

A week later I came across another limitation that took me totally by surprise. I was careening down a sidewalk while sightseeing and not paying attention to what was immediately in front of me. The root of a tree had grown under a slab of the sidewalk and had lifted it about three inches higher than the rest. I hit the barrier with such force that it stopped the wheelchair cold, and my upper body fell forward so that I was in effect "kissing my kneecaps." Once again, I was grateful for the seatbelt, otherwise I would have been sprawled out face-down on the sidewalk. I was really stuck and was helpless because I didn't have enough upper body strength to get back into an upright position. I was in that position for what seemed like hours before someone came along. A young Mexican woman was walking by, and I got her attention. She spoke no English, and I couldn't speak Spanish, so through a series of gestures and my crude attempt at Spanish, she was able to get the idea and assist me in sitting upright again. After thanking her profusely, I made my way back to the residence, paying attention to every crevice on the sidewalk.

  I asked someone to help me fashion two cloth loops that I had hung on the upper corners of the chair so that I could slip an arm through one at a time and start developing enough strength to pull my body upright should that situation ever happen again. I also started to use the universal gym in the garage on a regular basis to develop whatever little upper body strength I could. And it started to work. After a few weeks, the straps on the chair weren't necessary anymore. I could push my body up from my knees if I ever fell over again. I was so impressed with the universal gym and the fact that I could use it alone without any assistance that I bought one and donated it to the physical therapy department at St. Jude's Hospital as a way of thanking the staff and giving back.

  Every day was a new learning experience. It became a challenge for me to examine a newly discovered limitation or situation and try to figure out a way to accomplish the task. I also discovered that it was necessary for me to learn patience and to be as articulate as possible when directing a person who was helping me. I soon befriended one of the peer counselors at Winners, Tony Welch, who became a mentor as I ventured on the journey toward independent living. Tony had been a quadriplegic since the mid-1950s and shared with me many of the roadblocks he was confronted with post-injury.

I watched Tony like a hawk, observing every little detail of how he accomplished the daily humdrum tasks that we all do without a second thought—things we unconsciously take for granted. As I watched and learned, I began to dispose of many of the special attachments, gadgets, and utensils I was given during rehab. One of things that impressed me about Tony was his attitude, despite the obstacles he'd endured over the years. Tony had lost both legs at the hip because of pressure sores that had gotten out of hand. He put himself through school at USC long before there was public awareness about the disabled population. He married his high-school sweetheart, and they had a son who was getting ready to attend USC himself. Tony exhibited a really laid-back attitude and a true humility that was attractive to me.

There were three or four AA meetings a week within rolling distance, including meetings at an Alano Club called the "Snake Pit," so I was able to start regular attendance again. Buck would pick me up on Friday nights in the manual wheelchair, and we'd go to our home group in La Palma. It was great seeing the old gang again, and soon I was beginning to feel that I was finally participating in life again.

Buck suggested that I check out a meeting that was also in the vicinity and let him know what I thought. The meeting was called "Indian Charlie's," and it was one of the oldest meetings in the area. I rolled over to attend the meeting on a Wednesday night and was shocked at what I saw and heard.

It was a discussion meeting, and because I was new to the group, I decided to shut up and listen. One of the long-time attendees got up and slammed the Big Book onto the table, saying, "You don't need to take these damn steps. Just don't drink and go to meetings..." I was appalled at hearing this coming from the mouth of a person professing to have long-term sobriety. When I told Buck about it, he directed me to go to the meeting a few more times, regardless of my aversion to the group. I did and came away with a new appreciation for the amount of growth that occurred in me just because of the steps I'd taken up to that point in my life. Most of the people attending the meeting were still angry and not happy at all—but they were sober.

This reminded me of a conversation I once had with Frank about taking everyone's inventory in order to find out who the winners are—and it suddenly made sense! I had no desire to just exist and be miserable; I saw the results of that choice abruptly when attending that meeting.

I found myself in an embarrassing situation because of my quadriplegia at a large Sunday evening speaker meeting in Long Beach that Buck took me to. More than halfway through the meeting, I heard a strange noise coming from my body and suddenly smelled a foul odor. I leaned over to Buck and told him I thought I just had a "blow-out" in my pants. Buck got up and discreetly pushed me out to the parking lot to take me home. I was mortified when he transferred me into the car, getting feces all over his hands and the sheepskin seat covers. I tried to fight back the tears at the odiferous reminder that I had no control over my bowels. Buck tried to downplay the event as we drove down the freeway with the windows rolled down, saying that "everything would come out in the wash."

The next day I told Tony about the "blow-out" and asked him if this kind of thing ever happened to him. He told me from his own experience that if I watched my diet carefully and ate only one meal a day, two things would happen: I wouldn't gain a lot of weight because of my slow metabolism, and I would have a somewhat better measure of control over my bowel movements. I immediately started to pay attention to my diet to get a handle on the problem.

A few weeks later, Buck and I decided to make an excursion to the Seal Beach Sunday morning meeting we used to attend together. As it turned out, it was the hottest day of the summer. It was 104 degrees at the beach. A few people at the meeting who knew that I was coming had brought sheets of plywood and laid them out on the sand, allowing me to make my way to the parachute spread out on the beach without getting stuck.

Due to the spinal cord injury, I was aware of the fact that I couldn't sweat, allowing my body to cool off in the intense heat. I thought that two or three soda pops would be sufficient to keep me cool. As the day wore on, I began to feel really uncomfortable and extremely lightheaded. I didn't fully realize it at the time, but my body temperature was rising as the sun blazed upon the beach. Buck had to rush me home to Paramount with the AC on full blast in the car, where they discovered that my body temperature was 103 degrees. I was put in bed with cold compresses and ice to get my body temperature back to normal. Afterward, I've tried never to be out on a hot day again without a spray bottle of water and access to plenty of fluids to replenish my body.

Chapter 8
Learning to Take Responsibility and Beginning to Grow

"Made direct amends to such people wherever possible, except when to do so would injure them or others."
(Step 9 of Alcoholics Anonymous)

I was told to remove six words from my vocabulary at this point in the steps: "I'm sorry," "I apologize," and "yeah but." That was because the people in my life had been hearing those words come out of my mouth for years, yet my behavior never changed. People judge us not so much by what we say as by what we do. Only a consistent change of behavior on my part would convince the people still keeping me at arm's length that I was trying to be different.

In early July I was celebrating my thirty-second "belly-button" birthday. My sister Betty and sister-in-law Monique came to spend a week with me. I rented a midsize convertible for us to use and taught them how to transfer me into the front seat and how to fold up the manual wheelchair. The three of us were able to play tourist around southern California, going to places like Universal Studios and many other attractions, where we discovered it pays to hang out with a disabled person. We had great parking spots and were able to get on trams first that went around the complexes. We also went to the *Queen Mary* anchored in Long Beach harbor one night, where Betty and Monique dragged me out to the middle of the ballroom floor to dance with them.

During the course of the week, the girls went with me to some of the open AA meetings I attended at the time, and they were able to meet a lot of my friends. The time came when I had a private moment with Betty and was able to make amends to her. We had a long, tear-filled conversation about my inadequacies as an older brother. Every girl growing up with an older brother deserves to have someone that she can look up to and rely on to be there for her. Because of my selfish and self-centered nature, she was cheated out of that. I was a constant source of embarrassment for my family and anybody who was in the proximity of me during my drinking and using career. I knew that there was a lot of work ahead of me in order to make reparations for the damage that I had caused. I told Betty I would do whatever was necessary to right the wrongs I'd committed. Almost immediately, our relationship improved. At the end of the week, when the girls left to go to the airport, I thanked them for giving me the best week I'd had in a long time.

Later that month, my parents came to see how I was doing. They stayed at a motel a couple of miles from where I was living, and every morning I would roll over and spend the day with them. I was nervous and apprehensive because I knew the time had come to make amends, and I was fearful of the outcome. I finally summoned enough courage to do it and asked them to sit down for a moment because I needed to talk to them about something important. I'm so grateful that I was taught specifically how to make an amends to someone in a manner that didn't allow me any wiggle room in attempts at whitewashing or minimizing my behavior while under pressure. I learned how to thoroughly "clean my side of the street" to the best of my ability as I commenced making amends at every opportunity. Although the ninth step is my favorite, it's still the scariest because of what my mind tells me when I think of possible outcomes.

I started off by telling them that I was finally able to admit to myself that I was an alcoholic and had gotten involved in a 12-Step group that required me to take an honest, unvarnished hard look at myself and my behavior. I went on to say that not only was I a full-blown alcoholic, but my root problem was also the discovery that I was a liar, cheat, and thief as well. My parents, of course, tried to dismiss this description by telling me that I was just going through a phase. I asked them to just listen for a moment. I went on to explain many of my indiscretions. I told them that lying was my biggest character defect. I explained my motivations for lying and went on to tell them about the specific lies I remembered having told.

I also related that I always thought cheating was something like cheating at cards or on an exam at school, but it went far deeper than that. Every parent on this planet deserves to have a child that they can be proud of. I was a constant source of shame and embarrassment for my parents because of the trouble I caused in high school by leading student walkouts and getting suspended for a couple of weeks. I was also constantly appearing in the local newspaper because of arrests for marijuana and other illegal activities. For a while my father would get a phone call at 2:00 a.m. every Friday or Saturday and have to drive to the next town to bail me out of jail. My mother, for instance, was constantly cheated out of a good night's sleep because she was up worried about where her son was. My parents got ripped off.

I went on to talk about the material things I stole from them. I stole money from my mother's purse and checks from my father's safe in order to buy drugs and alcohol. I delved further into this by explaining that I took things from them that were priceless and intangible, like their time, their energy, their love, and affection, without ever giving thought to returning it in kind. I admitted that I was always a taker and until recently had never known about giving back without any strings attached.

I tried to make it clear to my parents that I wasn't looking for, nor did I expect their forgiveness. I was working hard on a daily basis not to be the same selfish, self-centered jerk they had always known. I told them that I loved them from the bottom of my heart, and I would do whatever was necessary to make up for the damage I'd caused in their lives. At this point, I needed to ask them two questions (I was taught that these questions were nonnegotiable):

1. Was there anything else that I had done to cause them harm or embarrassment that I wasn't aware of? (It was extremely important that I kept my mouth shut after this question. Being so self-absorbed, something that I thought was inconsequential might have devastated them, and this was their opportunity to let me know about anything I didn't remember or acknowledge)
2. What could I do to make things right? (If they told me to pound a tambourine at the airport for a year, I'd better put on a Hari Krishna outfit!)

When I asked the first question, my parents looked at each other and agreed that I'd been thorough, and they couldn't think of anything else. Their answer to the second question was the tallest order I've ever been given in my life. They simply said, "Keep doing what you're doing." My father came across the room, gave me a hug, and told me that he loved me very much. (Although I'm sure that he had uttered those words before, this was the first time I actually *heard* it coming from his lips.)

Note: From that point on, every time I've had the privilege of working with a newcomer or helping someone with the steps, I always had it in the back of my mind that it's a small way for me to make amends to my parents. There's no way I'm ever going to be able to balance the ledger, but I continue doing it anyway.

Over the next few months, as I *thought* I was completing my ninth step, I could feel myself growing by leaps and bounds, not only in dealing with my physical handicap, but more importantly, in my emotional and spiritual houses. Although I didn't fully realize it then, I began to vaguely understand that this step would be a major tool in helping me change my behavior as I humbled myself enough to sit in front of someone and admit my faults and character defects that caused so much harm in their lives. Forcing myself to do this wherever and whenever possible proved to be a deterrent against repeating the same actions, since it would require another amends down the road. It wasn't anywhere in my nature before this step to take full responsibility for the things I did. This process allowed some of the grime and grit clouding the facets of my "life stone" to clear as I worked and polished to improve its clarity, removing so many flaws as I came across them. I learned as the years went by that the ninth step will never be done because there are still people on my eighth step list of people that I haven't been able to locate. I don't know if they're alive or dead, but the willingness to make amends is always there, *no matter what.*

For example, years after being at Winners, I approached a Jaguar dealership I'd worked for to make amends and was able to speak directly to the owner, Dick. After talking for almost an hour about my many indiscretions and behaviors that almost caused him to lose his franchise license, it came to the moment of truth when I asked the two questions. Dick's response to the first question was that I was so thorough, he couldn't remember anything else. His answer to the second question floored me.

He said, "John, I'm sure that it took a lot of courage to do what you just did, but I've got to be honest with you—I don't recall half of the things you just told me about."

As we went our separate ways, I thought to myself, *Wow, if I'd known that, then I probably wouldn't have done this.* I knew deep in my heart that I still had to do it anyway because *I knew* what I'd done.

Winners had a shuttle vehicle that took residents on group outings to different venues or events, to individual medical appointments, and for us to run personal errands. I was able to have a staff member drive me once a week to spend an afternoon as a peer volunteer at the treatment center where I had gotten sober.

One day I was sitting in on a group session while the participants were performing an exercise I'd done as a patient. We took and numbered eight little pieces of paper. We were asked to write down the eight most important things in our lives at that time on each of the numbered pieces of paper. We were told that there were no right or wrong answers. When everyone was done, each person was asked to share with the group what was written as least important to them, wad it up, throw it into the trashcan, and really try to imagine what life would be like without it. As we worked our way to the most important things in our lives, the room got pretty sad. I had a lightning bolt of clarity strike me that afternoon when I realized that the word "sobriety," coincidently, has eight letters in it. If I lose any measure of the kind of sobriety I have, things on a list are meaningless because they'll eventually be gone anyway.

The weekly meetings with the Winners staff to gauge my progress started to become a mere formality. The staff helped me through conversations and through their examples to understand the concept that it's not important what a person has lost: it's what's left and what they do with it that really matters. Clarity began to form in my "life stone," little by little, without the blinding effects it once held…

Several of my friends made a point of learning the transfer technique so they could get me into their cars and take me to meetings. Although they had the best of intentions, I can't tell you how many evenings I was sitting on the front lawn waiting for the ride that never came. I made an earnest promise to myself (realizing that I'd been guilty of the same behavior) that in the future, if I ever committed to be someplace, I would be there unless my knees were nailed to the floor.

      The fall of 1988, I started driver's training. Because my left elbow is frozen at a ninety-degree angle, I required a pneumatic (air) system that had a hand control mounted on the door. I had no problem acclimating to the system, and after the initial two hours of orientation, I was chomping at the bit to get on the freeway again. I resisted the urge and slowed down, going through the entire driver's training process prescribed by the instructor. The afternoon I went to the DMV to renew my license, I met the examiner, who was almost old enough to be my grandmother. She seemed a little nervous when she saw the layout of the hand controls and the rest of the van I was using to take the test. I passed the test with flying colors, and the examiner said that I was the safest driver she'd ever tested. Afterward, I was in the parking lot blowing "snot bubbles" because I felt like a complete human being again! If you've never experienced this, it's when you have so many tears flowing, that bubbles are literally coming out of your nose. The following week, I ordered a new minivan to be modified and outfitted with the hand controls required.

Chapter 9
Learning, Growing, Despite Self-Will Running Amok

During one of the last weekly meetings at Winners, the staff unanimously told me that it was time to start looking for a place of my own because I'd surpassed the goals and objectives they set for me. I had conversations with the two attendants assigned to me, Rosa and Joyce, and made them offers to become my personal care attendants.

Buck and I decided to be roommates. Initially I thought about purchasing a house in Long Beach, but because my credit rating was in shambles, and the cost of renovations would have been so high, using all of my financial resources to make it happen was out of the question. I decided instead to look for rental property. I finally found a place in Huntington Harbor, a prosperous community in Huntington Beach. The house was on the canal, with a boat dock and swimming pool in the backyard. (Although I didn't realize it at the time, my grandiosity was coming into play one more time.) Buck and I moved into our new home on November 1, the day before my second AA birthday.

You don't *really* know a person until he or she lives with you for a while. I'd unwittingly put Buck on top of a pedestal and soon discovered he had flaws like anyone else. My new roommate, as it turned out, was a slob and was irresponsible when it came to putting things back where they belonged after using them, and I would mentally "screw myself up into the ceiling" because I was so mad. I overlooked these and his many other shortcomings because I loved him and knew that he put up with my faults as well.

Note: I learned, over the years, that if I'm pissed off at anyone, regardless of the situation, it's usually because I have been or am guilty of the same behavior.

Buck decided to retire from bricklaying and become a real estate agent again. He started a commercial development agency partnering with a retired developer he knew. I studied for a while to get my real estate license but decided it wasn't something I really wanted to do. I wanted to help Buck with his new venture, so I purchased a pristine two-year-old BMW 6 Series (which was the only thing Buck did keep immaculate) so he would look the part of a successful businessman. I bought Buck's old 260Z from him and sold it to Rosa, who promised to make payments as time went on while she was working for me. Buck, in kind, used his bricklaying talents to tile the inside of the shower in our new home, allowing me to roll the shower chair into it.

All was well for a time. Rosa worked for me during the week, and Joyce covered the weekend shifts. I soon got into a daily routine of getting up every morning and spending part of the day rolling around and exploring the new area, as well as going to the noon meeting at Thursday's, an old bar a few miles away that was converted to a meeting hall. I was amazed to find that the affluent neighborhood I lived in didn't have any curb cuts at intersections, so I had to go down driveways in order to cross the streets.

In mid-November, I received a phone call telling me that the van was almost completed. Joyce, the driving instructor who helped me get my license, and I made the road trip to Phoenix in his training van to complete the final fittings. The trip was only eight hours long. We arrived late in the evening and decided to go to the facility the next morning to check out my new van. When I saw it for the first time, I was floored; it was beautiful. Final fittings had to be done for the location of the hand control, wheelchair lock-down device, and the various other controls necessary for me to be an efficient driver. When all the adjustments were complete, a professional pin striper came in and did a job on the van that was truly elegant. This was my first brand new vehicle, and when I wrote the check to complete the purchase, my hand was shaking more than normal because it was the largest check I'd ever written…

The drive home was uneventful, other than getting used to the new hand controls. Shortly after I got home, I began to get out of control. I started doing things, despite the red flags waving in the back of my mind, that I *knew* I had no business doing. I was driving all over southern California, going to more meetings than usual and showing off the new van to my friends. I was up in my wheelchair sixteen to twenty hours a day while running amok. I was also going to the beach late at night without a jacket and caught a cold that quickly turned to pneumonia. I was rushed to the emergency room, where I stayed in ICU for a few days. After I was discharged, one of the doctors told me that pneumonia was the number one killer of quadriplegics and that I'd better change my habits if I expected to live long. For some reason, I didn't think the doctor's advice applied to me, so I went home and continued doing what I was doing...

I was back in the emergency room four days later. This time something was different between my ears. The doctors slipped what seemed like a small vacuum cleaner hose down my throat—I *knew* I was never going to see the sun rise again. For some reason, I wasn't afraid of dying, and the only thing going through my mind that evening was a short prayer: "Thy will be done, not mine." I *knew* without a doubt that my life was over, and I kept reciting the prayer in my mind until it became almost a mantra, and I finally drifted off to sleep. I woke up the next morning and was still breathing through the tube! A sense of peace and serenity wafted over me like none before, and I savored it with every fiber of my being, thanking God from the bottom of my heart for saving me one more time.

After almost two weeks in the hospital, I came home to face some startling revelations. Several thousand dollars had gone missing from my checking account. After further investigation, I discovered that Rosa was using my ATM card to withdraw money from the account. I'd mistakenly trusted her enough to give her the pin number so she could make withdrawals for me. I immediately fired her. While trying to repossess the 260Z I sold her, which she never made a payment on, I found out that I couldn't because the title was in her name. I changed the account and pin numbers to prevent any more theft.

Shortly before Christmas, Buck, Polly P., who had become a close friend, and I were talking about the fact that there was no big sober event in the area to celebrate New Year's Eve. We immediately got to work. With ten days to spare, we found an old hall to rent, got a sober band, and distributed flyers, having the idea that any leftover funds collected would be donated to Central Office. New Year's Eve found us loading the refrigerators with beverages and stocking counters with snacks, wondering if anybody would show up. By midnight the place was packed! There was even a little money to donate!

Note: The next year, we moved the party to a new, larger banquet hall that included a catered dinner and speaker meeting. followed by a dance. This tradition has continued to this day.

A week or so later, I was at a small afternoon discussion meeting I'd never been to before when I was totally blindsided. One by one, the attendees were sharing about what was going on in their lives as I sat next to a table, quietly sipping my cup of coffee. A young man who seemed very upset started talking about an old-timer who took him to his very first meeting. I listened intently as he described how this man not only became his sponsor who guided him through the steps but also his best friend, mentor, and father figure because he didn't have one growing up. The young man went on to talk about how his sponsor saved his life, and that he had died the day before. As he told us through his tears about how much he already missed his friend and how tough it was going to be to continue the journey of recovery without him, I felt a single tear roll down my cheek, followed by a stream… For the first time in my life, I was able to "get out of myself" long enough to actually *feel* someone else's pain. This was major growth for a guy like me who was always so self-absorbed. Compassion and empathy had taken root to eventually become an integral part of the man I am today.

During the first few months of 1989 I went through the process of finding and firing several personal care attendants. I was faced with some of the harsh realities related to the field. There is no licensure or certification required for attendant care, unless one goes through an agency and pays huge fees. Even though I offered a pay scale well above the norm, it became difficult to find people, with the exception of my weekend attendant, Joyce, who were reliable, trustworthy, and sensitive to my needs. I found a man through my former mentor at Winners who worked with quads as an LPN at the Long Beach VA Hospital. Rick worked for me about a year.

One day soon after he started began like any other. Rick helped me with my shower, and by this time I'd learned to shave and brush my teeth on my own. After getting dressed and having breakfast, we went our separate ways as I got into the van to go out and run some errands. I looked in the rearview mirror and noticed I was sitting a little lower than usual in my chair but didn't give it a second thought. I went to a meeting and hung out with some friends afterward. At one point, I leaned over and put my hand on the wheelchair cushion, finding that it was completely deflated. I called Rick, asking him to meet me at the house. We got me into bed and found a large area on my upper thigh that was completely black.

A 911 call got me to the hospital ER, where I was told the deflated cushion pushed my leg against the chair's metal frame, creating pressure on the outer part of my thigh that actually killed the tissue. I was surprised to learn that this happened over a period of approximately six hours. I was immediately scheduled for surgery, and a large portion of muscle was removed. I was sent home the next day and within an hour was bleeding profusely from my leg. I made another trip to the ER, and the doctors sutured a blood vessel that wasn't completely tied off during the first surgery. I'd forgotten what the nurses taught me at St. Jude's about the importance of constantly checking the cushion's pressure and tilting back in the chair on a regular basis to remove the weight from my bottom. The significance of this practice would come back to haunt me again to either get my attention or suffer the consequences.

Throughout all of this, Buck was going into the office every day, trying to get his business off the ground. Since he had no steady income, I took it upon myself to pay the household bills and keep my friend afloat financially. One afternoon, Buck and his partner came to me with a proposition. They had found a corner lot in Long Beach that used to be a gas station available at a "dirt cheap" price. The two went on to say that, because of the location, it could be flipped for more than twice the purchase price. They guaranteed that if I were to invest in the project, not only would I get my money back, but 50 percent of the profits when the property sold. They said that they'd need $275,000 from me so they could buy the lot. Startled, I explained to them that my money was tied up in CDs at the bank, and interest income was paying the $3,000 monthly rental payment on the house. Buck's partner explained that I could go to the bank and get a line of credit using the CD account as collateral and that their company would make the interest-only payments on the amount I borrowed until the property was sold. I told them that I needed a day or two to think about it.

The next day, I went to the bank to fully check out the possibilities of borrowing against my CD account and was told that it could be done without penalties as long as the interest-only payments were made. Even though my gut was warning me otherwise (red flag...), I filled out the necessary paperwork and received a check for $275,000. I didn't know it at the time, but I was the only investor in this scheme. I gave Buck the check and asked him to make sure that the interest payments were made. He promised me that they would be, and also that they'd get busy marketing the property.

Once again the "ism" (incredibly short memory) I suffer from came into play, and I paid the price. You'd think that a near-death experience like the one I had with the pneumonia episode would have a lasting effect on my behavior. I was once again spending an average of eighteen hours a day in my wheelchair without tilting, as I was taught. (Imagine yourself sitting on a cement park bench for even six hours and not having the ability to flinch any of your muscles or move at all. Wouldn't you be in pain after a while?) I spent so much time in the wheelchair, not paying attention to the signals my body was trying to send me, that pressure sores developed on my rear end. I had to go into the hospital to have several "skin flap" operations to repair the damage I caused.

After the surgeries, I was transferred to a convalescent hospital so I could recuperate. I found myself ogling the nurses because I hadn't been with a woman since I got sober. This preoccupation with the nurses was only made worse because I was able to have erections and was helpless to do anything about them. One afternoon I found myself praying to God, asking for one of the nurses to come into my room and molest me that night. Within twelve hours of uttering that prayer, a nurse did come in and molest me, however, the nurse was the wrong sex.

The next morning I called my friend Polly and explained what happened. She told me to call the police because, in effect, I'd been raped. I did what Polly suggested, and the police arrived to take my statement. The local district attorney couldn't prosecute the male nurse because it was my word against his. The hospital administration dismissed the man until my stay was over.

Buck came to see me later that afternoon, and, expecting some sympathy or empathy on his part, I was surprised when he asked. "What part did you play in it?" I was shocked—of course I'd been praying to God to have a nurse come in and molest me because I was lonely and had a bad case of "monk madness," but that wasn't the real deal. After thinking about it for a few days, I realized that I did play a major part in it.

There is a line in the Big Book that states (on page 62) "...we invariably find that at some time in the past we have made decisions based on self that later put us in a position to be hurt." I was amazed at the epiphany I had during my soul searching. My behavior in the previous months had the cause and effect that the book talked about. If I'd been doing what the nurses in rehab taught me, I wouldn't have spent so much time in the wheelchair, only to have mutilated my rear end. So if I'd been doing what I should've been doing in the first place, I wouldn't have put myself in a position to be hurt. This was both a staggering and humbling admission to swallow and accept. Another fault in my "life stone" was revealed: I was operating with my self-will running riot, without any thought of a price to be paid then or later, and sober at the same time! I came to grips with the fact that I needed to go "back to basics," or it was going to kill me. I also learned the hard way that you've got to be careful what you pray for because you just might get it. I decided to keep things simple, and instead of praying for my own selfish ends, I would only use the third and seventh step prayers to start my days.

I spent two more months in the hospital, and by the time I got home, something had changed in my demeanor. A few of my friends made comments about how quiet, introspective, and spiritual I seemed to be around them. The truth was deep inside me. I was so ashamed of and disgusted with my recurring character defects that I couldn't find the words to explain how I felt. I vaguely sensed that somehow I was reaching another plateau in my laborious search for spiritual growth.

This was to be challenged a few days later when Buck brought me some disturbing news. He and his partner hadn't been careful enough in checking everything related to the lot purchased six months earlier. As it turned out, the soil was contaminated because of a leaking underground fuel tank, and the cleanup costs would far outweigh any profit they hoped to make. I calmly told Buck to find a way to unload the property as is because I wasn't going to invest another dime in the project.

By the time I got the proceeds from the sale of the property, it was less than half of the original investment. I also found out that none of the interest-only payments on the credit line were made at all. I drove to the bank, deposited the check I was given, paid the penalties, and after the dust settled, there was about one-third of the original CD investment left in the account. I told Buck to sell off the BMW, and I'd give him $2,000 so he'd be able to get another car. I also told him to find a new place to live as soon as possible because I was *done*. The BMW sold for about half of what I originally paid for it, which only added salt to my wounds. By the time Buck did leave two weeks later, we weren't talking to each other at all. I was so angry at being taken advantage of that I couldn't bring myself to say anything to him because I didn't want to say something I'd regret later.

Rick finally told me that working two jobs was taking a toll on him and his family life, so he suggested that I start looking for a new attendant. I appreciated his candor and began a search for someone to help me during the week.

After the experience with the male nurse, I began to worry about what I was able to do sexually. One afternoon I called one of my "road dog" friends, Marshall, and sheepishly asked him how to find a hooker because I'd never done that kind of thing before. Marshall told me to look in the newspaper under the personal ads and what to ask for. I was extremely embarrassed but finally made the call. I explained exactly what I was looking for, and an appointment was made for later that evening. Ron, an attendant I'd recently hired, let the woman into the house when she arrived as he left for the evening. The woman told me to call her Trish and asked what I needed. I shyly explained that I was trying to find out what worked and what didn't. I found out that no matter what we did, I couldn't achieve an erection. When she left that evening, she gave me her personal number and asked me to call her whenever I wanted to.

The AA world is small, and it seemed that everyone knew I had a major resentment with Buck, although they didn't know the details. One Monday night while at a meeting, "Big Bob" G. approached me and suggested that I pray for Buck. I told Bob that there was no way in hell that I'd pray for that asshole. Bob grinned and reminded me of the story in the Big Book titled "Freedom from Bondage." Bob suggested that every night for two weeks I should pray for Buck by first of all telling God exactly what I thought of him, even if it took a half an hour to get it off my chest, and then, whether I meant it or not, utter the words "I wish him health, wealth, and happiness." I respected Bob enough to know that he'd never steer me in the wrong direction. I promised Bob that I would force myself to do exactly what he asked. When I voiced the last words of that prayer for Buck, of course, I didn't mean it, by any stretch of the imagination.

After about a week of this, without realizing it, my attitude started to change. My mind slowed down enough to look at the part I played in the entire fiasco. Nobody twisted my arm to get involved in the "get rich quicker" proposal. It actually was my grandiosity and greediness that motivated me to get involved in the first place. After about three weeks of praying, it seemed as if a miracle happened. I attended the usual Thursday night Seal Beach meeting and was able to sit next to Buck without a single hair standing up on the back of my neck. The resentment was gone! Bob was right, after all.

It was time to sign a new lease agreement for the home in Huntington Harbor. After looking at my dwindling finances, I realized I couldn't afford to continue living there. I talked to the owners, and after I explained my situation, they allowed me to stay there on a month-to-month basis until I could find a new place to live. I scoured the newspapers and came across an ad for a rental property in Huntington Beach that included an option to buy. After meeting the owner and looking at the house, I negotiated a one-year lease with the option to buy it afterward.

Before moving into the new place, I hired a contractor to make some minor changes so that the entire first floor was accessible. I also had him install an intercom between the front door and the master bedroom. The house had a second-floor apartment with a private entrance that I rented out to a girlfriend of one of the "road dogs." The 3,000-square-foot dwelling also had a swimming pool in the backyard as well as a barbecue pit.

Life was good for a while after I moved into the new house in the beginning of 1990 having it set up just the way I wanted. That summer, my parents and my sister Linda, along with her son and daughter, came to visit for a week. We had fun going to local attractions like Disneyland, Knott's Berry Farm, as well as Universal Studios. Everyone had a blast especially, J.J., my slightly autistic nephew. He really loved riding on the back of his uncle's wheelchair as we went around the attractions.

One afternoon, after one of our treks, I had a moment to myself in the backyard. I suddenly realized what day it was, and tears started streaming down my face. Mom came out, and seeing me crying, she thought that something was wrong. I explained to her that there wasn't anything wrong—I was crying tears of joy because it was the third anniversary of the car accident, and I was happy just to be sucking air.

After everyone left, I started to call Trish on a regular basis. She introduced me to one of her girlfriends in case she wasn't available. Once again, I became obsessed and spent thousands of dollars trying to feel better about myself. Things got so out of hand that I even had one of the girls come and see me late one evening in a hospital room during a routine stay. I finally came to the conclusion that I couldn't participate in casual or sport sex, since I had a propensity for "falling in love" as I was giving the girls $200 an hour. I started to ask myself the question: *How pathetic are you, dude?* Alcoholics seem to have trouble in two areas in their life after sobering up—finance and romance—and I was no exception…

Chapter 10
Hidden Motives—Even from Ourselves as We Try to Grow Up

Within a week of Buck moving out of the Huntington Harbor home, I asked Joe R. to be my sponsor. Joe was a member of my home group, and we'd become friends over the years. I always admired the serene demeanor that Joe exhibited when we were together. I wanted what he had and knew it was only going to happen if I continued working on the steps with some guidance. I looked at my eighth list again and got back to work on the ninth step.

One of the more emotionally difficult amends I made was to Buzz because he'd put so much trust in me. Although I'd worked for him for three years, I only stole from him once. One Sunday afternoon, I was in the shop working on my car when someone came in with a Fiat that had a broken ball joint. I used a replacement part that was in stock and charged the person for the repair. I gave Buzz back the money for the part, as well as the money I collected for the repair in order to make things right.

Surprising things started happening as I went through the amends list. The people I'd listed as "maybe" moved into the ASAP column. And some on the never list slowly started to edge their way into that column as well. I became even more willing to clean up the messes I had caused in people's lives without even realizing it.

One night a few years later, I was attending a men's "twelve-and-twelve" meeting. This type of meeting studies the book *Twelve Steps and Twelve Traditions*. We happened to be on the eighth step. During the course of the discussion, I happily reported that there were no more "maybes" or "nevers" on my list. Halfway through the meeting, I realized that the statement was in fact a lie and immediately stuck up my hand and told the guys the truth.

The one amends still in my never column concerned a Jaguar dealership I used to work at, and it was of a financial nature. I was the only Jaguar technician there and had ten bays at my disposal. Usually, only two of the slots were occupied by legitimate customers' cars, and the rest were occupied with "side jobs" that I was doing under the table. I had no idea how many thousands of dollars I stole from the dealership, and that was one of the many reasons why this particular amends was squirreled away in the far right column so I wouldn't have to own up to it.

After the meeting, many of the men whom I admired and considered mentors came to me suggesting that if I were to be truly free, I was going to have to make this amends as soon as possible. I went home that night with a lot to think about and prayed on it until I fell asleep…

I woke up the next morning with a resolve to take care of it. I was willing to pay the dealership $100 a month for the rest of my life if that was what it took to make things right again. I picked up the "six-hundred-pound phone" and called the dealership, asking to speak to Ray, the owner. I identified myself to his secretary and told her that I needed to speak to Ray on a matter of a personal nature. She put me on hold for a moment and came back on the line to say that Ray was currently on a hunting trip in Montana, and could she put me in touch with the VP of the company? I thought to myself that I owed the amends to the company, so I gave her my phone number and was assured that I'd hear from someone later that morning.

A few hours later, I received a call from a gentleman named Mike, the VP. His voice sounded strangely familiar. When asked about the nature of my earlier call, I told him that I needed to talk about some things that went on while I was employed there and asked for an appointment to see him that afternoon. We agreed to meet. I asked Mike if we knew each other, since his voice was so recognizable, but I couldn't quite put my finger on it.

Mike replied, "Sure you know me. I was the parts manager when you worked here!" When the phone call ended, I slapped myself on the forehead. There was *another* amends I had to make because I always went out of my way to make his life miserable when I worked there—more was revealed.

I arrived at the dealership a half hour early, and it took me twenty minutes of sitting in the van to pull it together. Although I'm paralyzed from the chest down, it felt as if my knees were knocking because I was so afraid of what was about to happen. After what seemed an eternity, I finally exited the van to meet Mike.

He was a little shocked to see me in a wheelchair, so as we went to his office, I explained the circumstances and did my best to put him at ease. When we entered the office, I got down to business... I told him that I'd finally admitted to my *innermost* self that I was an alcoholic, and Mike nodded and said he knew that. I've always been amazed that this admission has never surprised anyone I've made amends to. We think we're so good at hiding it. I started to talk about the numerous lies I had told in order to cover my tracks while engaging in unethical behavior during the time I was employed there, and he replied that they always suspected I was never on the "up and up."

I had the nickname "Jaguar John" long before I came to AA—it originated at the dealership because of my affinity for driving customers' cars home at night under the pretense of a "test drive," when I was really joyriding. I went on to say that the dealership was cheated out of having an honest and trustworthy employee because I always spent the majority of my time thinking about devious methods of making money. When I told Mike about all of the "side jobs," as well as the parts I stole, he merely nodded and stated that they assumed I was doing something underhanded but could never catch me in the act.

It took everything I had in me to tell him that, although I had no way of knowing how much I stole from the company, I was more than willing to do whatever was necessary to square up the debt. Then I asked the first question. Mike thought for a moment and said, "Well, as a matter of fact there is. The last side job you did here before you left was a total engine overhaul on a little green MGB. A few weeks after you were gone, the engine blew up, and the owner took us to court. We ended up paying her $3,500." My heart sank as I thought, *Okay, $100 a month for two lifetimes...*

Before the conversation could continue any further, two Honda mechanics came in to talk to Mike about vehicles they were working on. When asked if they remembered me, they looked at him quizzically until Mike reminded them of the MGB incident. They instantly remembered me, and I wanted to crawl under a rock to die. As the guys and I began to reminisce, Mike excused himself for a moment to take care of a situation in the shop. He returned and the guys went back to work, wishing me well. I thought to myself as I sucked it up, *This is where the rubber meets the road* and asked Mike the final question, bracing myself for the answer...

Mike smiled slightly and explained to me that he hadn't been in the shop taking care of a problem. He was, in fact, in Ray's office talking to him about the conversation we just had. As it turned out, Ray was not on a hunting trip in Montana. When his secretary told him that I was on the phone wanting to talk earlier that day, he remembered what a lowlife I was and didn't want to speak to me but was intrigued about what I wanted and was listening to our entire conversation on the intercom! Mike went on to say, "John, as far as Ray is concerned, we're even-steven. The fact that you came in and copped to all the stuff you did showed us something we swore we'd never see in someone like you—courage, character, and integrity. So go and have a good life, buddy."

I stammered as I said good-bye and was stunned while making my way out to the van. At one point I had to pull off the freeway because I couldn't see where I was driving due to the river of tears streaming down my face. I was crying not because "I got off"; I was more than willing to make payments for the remainder of my life. Someone used the words *courage, character,* and *integrity* in the same sentence with my name in it...

It's ironic that the "twelve-and-twelve" mentions "finding love on the AA campus," because it happened to me shortly after my family went back to their homes. I met Stephanie at a meeting one night, becoming friends with her almost immediately. I was shocked one evening when she asked me out on a date. The Grand Prix of Long Beach was running that weekend, and she had friends who owned an apartment in one of the towers along the racecourse. She told me that we'd be able to see the entire race with a bird's-eye view. I was so excited at the prospect of actually going out on a real date that I pushed and hurried Joyce while getting ready to go that morning. Unknowingly, I had a kink in my catheter that would prove to be disastrous later in the day.

When we got to the apartment in the tower, I was out on the balcony watching the cars go by and drinking plenty of fluids because it was a hot day. Within an hour I started to sweat profusely, and my head pounded because my blood pressure was raised significantly. I knew there was something wrong because I was experiencing autonomic disreflexia. I motioned Stephanie aside, telling her that I had to leave. She looked at me quizzically and after a moment agreed. Almost immediately after dropping her off, I urinated through my penis, soaking my jeans, and was mortified. I called Joyce on the car phone, asking her to meet me at the house because I needed help. When we met, the kink was found and I felt like a complete idiot. Surprisingly enough, my screw-up didn't seem to put Stephanie off, since we continued to see each other.

One afternoon, I received a call from her asking for help because the car she was driving at the time broke down. The engine in her little Chevette was destroyed, and it was going to cost more money to fix than it was worth. She was working for a temp agency and didn't have any money or the credit rating to buy another vehicle. I called Buzz to see if he had any vehicles for sale. He had a small Fiat 131 that would fit the bill, so I bought the car from him and gave it to Stephanie. I didn't realize it at the time, but I was backsliding into old behaviors once again—buying affection because the sex was great and I didn't want her to leave.

The vehicle had a few minor electrical problems that she constantly whined and complained about. I would have Buzz fix them as they came up. It got to the point where I was tired of hearing about it and started looking for another car. I found a used Mercedes Benz that was in reasonably good shape. I told Stephanie that I would cosign a loan for her to purchase the car so she could get her credit rating back in order. This time I used a little common sense and secretly had an extra key made, just in case. I took the little Fiat and sold it to my "road dog" friend Marshall, who promised to make payments. He never made one, leading me to learn that expectations are really nothing more than "premeditated resentments."

Soon after moving into the new two-story house, I started to have a feeling that I somehow needed to make a contribution to the community. I decided to open a business selling and repairing minivans that were outfitted for disabled individuals. I experienced one of those epiphanies about perceptions after filing a DBA in the local newspaper and going to the Huntington Beach City Hall to get an operating permit. I went with one of my "road dog" buddies, Joe M., to get the applications. Both Joe and I were dressed casually in jeans when we went to City Hall that afternoon. After being in the line for a while, we made it to the counter, and something unusual happened. Even though I was the person applying for the permit, the woman behind the counter was asking Joe questions all about my business idea, ignoring the fact that I was right in front of her! Joe was as confused as me, and I finally asked the woman for the necessary paperwork, telling her that it would be brought back later. As we were driving back to my place, I had a brainstorm and asked Joe to participate in an experiment when we returned.

When we went back to file the paperwork the next day, I purposely wore a shirt and tie, while Joe wore jeans. As luck would have it, the same woman was at the counter. Without prompting from either of us, the woman addressed me directly this time, going through the details to make it official that I now owned a small business. Her demeanor was professional and respectful—the total opposite of the previous encounter. A lesson was learned about perceptions that would aid me the rest of my life.

My house wasn't very far from Buzz's home, so one day I decided to take a chance and drive over to talk with him about sharing the new shop he had just opened. He agreed that it would help us both out if we shared the rent and the overhead. About a week later, I moved into his shop, splitting the office space with him, and started to sell minivans while using the company that I originally purchased my van from as a source. My van was constructed shortly after the prototype was completed and had many glitches that needed to be ironed out. Every time it broke down, I made the van more reliable with each repair. I went to Phoenix for training seminars and shared the modifications I made on the van with them. I soon began to feel the same sense of gratification I would get when I successfully repaired a vehicle before the accident.

One afternoon, I was getting ready to make another road trip to Phoenix. As Ron was packing up the van, I received a call from Stephanie with what felt like a final nail in the coffin when she said, "Let's just be friends." Ron and I got into the loaded van and started heading out. My mind was racing as I crossed the desert, not paying any attention to how fast I was going. I looked up into the rearview mirror and saw flashing red lights. The highway patrolman who stopped me said that he clocked me doing in excess of 120 miles per hour. He went on to explain that normally when someone was going that fast, the police would impound the car and put the driver in jail. He looked at me in the wheelchair and decided it wasn't worth calling the paddy wagon out to the middle of the desert and heat to haul me away. He gave me a firm warning and wrote the ticket for 85 miles per hour. The rest of the trip I went the speed limit although my mind was still racing at light speed.

When we finally got to the hotel room, the first thing I did was call the local AA central office to find a meeting. The meeting I found was in a small hole-in-the-wall building in nearby Tempe. There were possibly a dozen people in the meeting, and surprisingly enough, a newcomer who grew up in Huntington Beach was in attendance. He had tried to get sober at some of the same meetings that I went to. It was as if God answered my prayer because I was able to focus on helping someone rather than feeling sorry for myself. After a good night's sleep, I awoke fresh, relaxed, and ready to do what I there for in the first place.

Within a week after I returned from the road trip, the bank informed me that Stephanie hadn't made a payment on the Mercedes in four months. I grabbed Ron as well as the spare key and went to the parking lot where she worked to repossess the car. She called me later, thinking that the car was stolen. When I told her that I took it and why, she went off... My voice was calm as I told her that real "friends" don't take advantage of each other in this way. I was done with her. I went to the bank, withdrew money, and again paid the penalties from my dwindling CD account in order to pay off the car loan.

For the next few weeks, it seemed as if I was in a fog—sober. I wasn't able to keep focused on anything because the cavern between my ears was jam-packed with a huge number of negative voices constantly beating me up for repeating the same behavior over and over again—always thinking that the outcome would be different this time. Isn't this one of the many definitions of *insanity*? The voices were in a screaming contest, all aimed at trying to get my attention first by asking things like "You're a useless, pathetic, and worthless excuse for a man—who could possibly love a guy like you that's in a wheelchair anyway? What good are you, really, aside from a bank account?" I talked to Joe about how bad it was, but it didn't help. One afternoon while driving to work, the voices in my head got so loud and overpowering that I had to do something. I turned the van around and went to a meeting.

I arrived about an hour early and met a woman there who was setting up the meeting. She had about twenty-five years of sobriety. She took one look at me and asked what was wrong, and I came unglued. I started crying, telling her the whole sordid episode and about the voices that were yelling between my ears. She hugged me, gave me a sheet of paper from her purse, and suggested that I read it out loud every morning to help deal with what she called "silly nonsense." As she went back to setting up the meeting, I read what I was given as my head and heart calmed down a bit. I continued reading it for a while, until the pain lessened and eventually it fell to the wayside.

One of the names on my amends list was Sally because of the way I'd treated her when our relationship ended. She accepted my amends and suggested that we start over with a clean slate, so we started seeing each other again. Without realizing it, I was once again backsliding into old behaviors and MOs by paying off some of her bills, giving her the Mercedes, and even cosigning a consolidation loan for her. One evening she came over to spend the night, and as we kissed, I was shocked at the taste of alcohol on her breath! I'd assumed that she'd been sober since her stay at the treatment center. Once again, red flags started flying that I chose to ignore.

People say that love is blind, but because of my experience, it's really lust. I was so enamored with our relationship (more to the point—the sex) that I continued to see her in spite of what I *knew* intellectually; there wasn't anything I could do to fix her. I finally saw what was really happening and walked away.

I recalled the woman with twenty-five years of sobriety who gave me the paper to be read on a daily basis when I was hurting so badly because of the breakup with Stephanie. I went into my bedroom, found it, and upon reading it again, I decided to put it in a place where I'd see it every morning and read out loud, as she suggested to me in the first place:

On His Plan for Your Mate

Everyone longs to give themselves completely to someone to have a deep soul relationship with another, to be loved thoroughly and exclusively. God says, "No, not until you are satisfied and fulfilled and content with living loved by me alone, with giving yourself totally, unreservedly with me alone. I love you my child and until you discover that only in me is your satisfaction to be found, you will not be capable of the perfect human relationship that I have planned for you. You will never be united with another, until you are united with me... exclusive of anyone or anything else, exclusive of any other desires and longings. I want you to stop planning, stop wishing and allow me to give you the most thrilling plan existing... one that you can't imagine. I want you to have the very best. Please allow me to bring it to you. Just keep your eyes on me, expecting the greatest things... Keep experiencing that satisfaction knowing that I AM. Keep learning and listening to the things I tell you. You must be patient and wait. Don't be anxious... don't worry... don't look around at the things others have gotten or that I've given to them. Don't look at the things you think you want. Just keep looking to me, or you will miss what I want to give you. And then, when you are ready, I will surprise you with a love far more wonderful than you could ever dream. You see, until you are ready and until the one I have for you is ready, I am working even this very minute to have both of you ready at the same time. Until you are both satisfied exclusively with me and the life I have prepared for you, you won't be able to experience the love that exemplifies your relationship with me and this perfect love. And dear one, I want you to have this most wonderful love. I want you to see in the flesh a picture of your relationship with me, and to enjoy materially and concretely the everlasting union of beauty and perfection. I am God Almighty. Believe and be satisfied. "

I started to read this every morning and concentrated on helping others, and I ended up staying celibate for over two years. Had I known that would've happened, chances are I wouldn't have been so diligent about reading and applying it.

I also took a look at my financial status, and for the first time in a long time, I experienced a sense of dread and fear. The CD account in the bank expired, with only $60,000 left that I deposited into my checking account. It had taken a few years for me to completely burn through more than half a million dollars. The only things I had left were the van, a house full of furniture, and some gym equipment to show for the small fortune I initially deposited in the bank. I was sickened to the core, and every fiber of my being was in agony because of the undeniable truth I'd just swallowed. I tried to make myself feel better by thinking that I helped a lot of people.

Note: When I honestly took a look at my real motives, I was ashamed to admit that I wasn't the altruistic person I put up the front to be—everything I did was so that people would think I was a great guy. My selfish and self-centered nature surfaced once again, making me believe all the lies I told myself one more time.

Out of desperation and fear, I started to work overtime at building the business, trying to make it a success. I used every marketing tool I could think of to sell minivans to individuals and municipalities. The hours I put into these efforts took a toll on my body, and I ended up in the hospital again for a month. When I was finally discharged from the hospital, I made a decision to move again in order to lessen my overhead.

During the first five years of my sobriety, I became good friends with Bill B., who I met at the Tuesday-night meeting held at the hospital where we both got sober. Bill heard about my need to lessen my overhead, and because he was having roommate problems, he asked me about becoming roommates. It seemed like a great idea to me, so we started looking around. We found a modest three-bedroom house in Huntington Beach for rent at a price that would benefit us both. When we made the move, the storage facility that I had was packed with even more stuff because we both had houses full of furniture.

As soon as I completed the move, I called the Dayle McIntosh Center in Anaheim for help in finding a new attendant because Ron hadn't worked out. I talked to a gentleman named Peter who referred me to Hector, a man that worked for him on the weekends and was quite reliable. I interviewed Hector and hired him on the spot. We became fast friends and worked well together.

I've always thought it was ironic that the admonishments Fred gave me when I was six months sober about not having any business sponsoring anyone until I had five years of sobriety became true without any help from me. Fred came over to me in 1991, when I was taking a cake at the Thursday night Seal Beach meeting to celebrate my fifth AA birthday and told me to listen carefully for the pop. "What pop?" I asked.

Fred laughed and said, "The pop occurs when your head comes out of your ass." I have yet to hear the pop. Soon afterward, men were coming out of the woodwork, asking me to sponsor them. I've always laid out the ground rules—just as my first sponsor did for me—but have also made it abundantly clear that I am not a marriage counselor, employment officer, or financial adviser because of my own track record. I would be willing to help them take the steps as I was taught.

Note: One of the things I've been also known to do when working with a man for a while who has taken a few of the steps takes place when we're talking and he's complaining about something not going his way in life. When he's finished, I'll just smile and say, "Thanks for helping me stay sober today, dude—because that's the saddest story I've ever heard!" It's because he forgets who he's talking to...

My sponsor Joe and I had a tough time getting together due to work schedules and the distance between our homes, so I asked Alton for help. He had thirty-five years of sobriety and a story that was truly inspirational. He was a wino in New Orleans who couldn't read or write. He taught himself to read by becoming "a student" of the Big Book. Alton always had the dream of being a poet and eventually had his poetry published.

Despite Alton's suggestion that it wasn't a wise idea to hire Joe, my "road dog" buddy from the city hall episode, I did it anyway because I wanted to give the man a chance. Joe had recently gotten loaded again and was newly sober. He was also a motorcycle mechanic and possessed the aptitude needed to make repairs on some of the vehicles that came into the shop for work. I offered Joe the job, and because he didn't have a place to live, I offered to let him stay in the extra bedroom that Bill and I had.

One afternoon at the shop, while I was on the phone in the office, my minivan needed to be moved to make room for a customer's vehicle. Joe moved it for me, and instead of using the brake and gas pedals, he decided to show off by using the hand controls to move my demo vehicle. He lost control of the van and crashed it into a freshly painted Mercedes and Buzz's El Camino. The crashing of the cars could be heard throughout the entire shop. When I came out of the office and saw all the damage, I asked Joe what he was thinking. He didn't have a reasonable explanation. I made a call to my insurance company and was told that once the $1,000 deductible was met, all three cars would be repaired. I knew Joe didn't have that kind of money and told him that I'd take care of it. I fired him, telling him he had to find a different place to live. Once Alton got wind of what happened, he told me to find a new sponsor because I wasn't willing to follow directions. That floored me, but I knew he was right.

The next day I had a long talk with Buzz, explaining the financial mess I'd put myself in and that I had to close the minivan business. I told him that I wasn't in a position to share the overhead with him any longer. He said not to worry about it because he'd been looking for a new location for a few months and found the perfect place. He told me that it was all working out for the best. He wished that I'd come to him earlier and maybe he could've helped. When the subject of Sally came up, Buzz said he suspected that she was probably a gold digger from the start, especially after the episode he and his wife Janet had with her while I was in the hospital.

When I got home that night, Bill and I had a conversation lasting into the wee hours of the morning. I was beating myself up because I still suffered in a major way from selfishness, self-centeredness, grandiosity, self-pity, lust, self-delusion, and a lot of other things that made me sick. Bill reminded me that just because we were sober, there wasn't any way we would ever become saints or see through other people's motives or even ours at times, for that matter. Our thinking became so distorted over the years, and it wasn't going to change overnight. I had to admit that I'd better start focusing on growing up.

A few weeks later, I came home to find Bill sitting on the couch with a concerned look on his face. He told me that we needed to talk. Bill said that he needed to invest in a condo or possibly a house because his ex-wife was trying to take him for everything he was worth. I knew that he went through a rather nasty divorce, and his ex-wife was constantly hounding him. He was wealthy at one time, but toward the end of his drinking career he found it more comfortable to live in the bushes in a park rather than in his two-million-dollar home with his family. Bill asked me, if he were able to purchase a new place, if I would still want to be his roommate. I told him that of course I would because that's what friends do.

Within a few weeks, he purchased a condo in Fullerton through our mutual friend and real estate agent Jackie. It was only about four miles from where Hector lived, so it was convenient for everyone. I moved into the downstairs master bedroom that had a bathroom attached to it, and Bill took the two bedrooms upstairs, which also had a bathroom. During the move, I deposited all of my furniture and things, with the exception of the bedroom set, in the storage facility I'd been renting for some time.

Chapter 11
Still Growing up a Micron at a Time

"Continued to take personal inventory and when we were wrong promptly admitted it."
(Step 10 of Alcoholics Anonymous)

Note: It's just my opinion—so you can take it for what it's worth—that the tenth, eleventh, and twelfth steps are what I call "quality control steps," because they've helped me greatly, acting, most importantly, as deterrents against repeating some of the most glaring and hurtful character flaws I'd been guilty of for so many years. The tenth step has been a "filter," so to speak. Most of the time, when my head tells me to do something inappropriate, I don't act on it. But I'm human and still make mistakes from time to time. The last two steps aid in my spiritual growth and keep me on the path. It took a long time, coupled with work and patience (mostly with myself) to come to this conclusion...

Through the process of taking the first nine steps, I learned that the quality personality traits I admired in other people from a distance were inside of me all along. They were actually hidden behind the huge inclusions in my "life stone" that made me sick as I was discovering them in myself. Inclusions are characteristics that occur inside a stone. They are usually called flaws because their presence means the stone is nowhere near perfect. They are like fingerprints, a characteristic that gives us all a special signature. Getting to know your "life stone" inside and out as you remove and smooth the rough edges makes it even more priceless although its' worth is intangible to the outside world. One of my goals then and now is to be totally transparent in every area of my life, despite my many flaws.

The last minivan I sold before closing the business down was to a woman who became paralyzed as a result of a botched surgery. When we went through the list of options available, she ordered all the "bells and whistles" available, including a custom sunroof. Even though I only required half of the purchase price, she insisted on paying for the van in its entirety. I reluctantly accepted her check, ordering the van through my source in Phoenix, and sent them half of my cost for the vehicle. When the van was completed, it was delivered to me, and I paid them the balance due. The only detail left was to take it to a local shop and have the sunroof installed. There was a problem, however: I'd mismanaged her funds and didn't have the money to pay for it. I stalled her for a few weeks while trying to "rob Peter to pay Paul" and get the installation paid for. Bill lent me the money to get the minivan from the sunroof shop. I bit the bullet, humbling myself when I delivered the minivan, and told her the truth about why it took so long to get it to her. She was extremely angry and had every right to be. She called me names that made me blush with embarrassment, telling me to get off of her property and never to come back.

Until I started the dealership, I had no medical insurance and had to rely on Medicare for my health care needs. After operations began, I found a small business plan that provided quality affordable insurance for up to ten people. I signed up for it and invited several of my friends to join me that were in the same predicament. Every month they'd send me their premium payments, and I would forward a single check to the insurance company. As you can probably imagine, about a year later, I screwed up one more time, falling behind on the payments and putting everyone in danger of losing their coverage. I called the agent who originally set up our plan and learned about a new program that allowed everyone to have individual plans without a monthly price increase provided I paid the amount owed. I went to everyone involved and admitted my fault, promising to get their accounts up to date so they could take advantage of the new program. Many good relationships I had were destroyed because of my lack of trustworthiness when it came to money matters.

In order to straighten out the financial mess I'd created for myself and for others, I took out a loan on my van. I caught up on everyone's premiums as I had promised, and nobody lost their coverage. But as usual, I eventually fell behind on the high interest payments for the van, only to have it repossessed. Not knowing what to do, I talked to my friends Bob S. and Tom T., and they came up with an idea. Tom was refurbishing a 1950s

Greyhound bus to make a custom motor home and could use specialty tools to complete the project. I made a deal with Tom to sell him all of my tools. We met at Bob Gillespie's house, who was storing the tools for me, in order to complete the transaction. Tom gave me the agreed upon cash so that I could take possession of my van once again. At last the van was paid off, and, other than regular monthly obligations, my head was above water. I thanked God that my attorney Don had the foresight to set me up with a tax-free income for life, now that most of my assets were all but gone. I learned something about myself and found yet another flaw in my "life stone" that was pretty painful to swallow—it took every nickel of the $650,000 I had in the bank at one time for me to learn that I didn't know how to manage money...

I'd been going to the Wednesday night meeting on Heil Street in Huntington Beach for some time. I met Dick E. and watched him interact with other members of the group. Soon I befriended Dick and asked him to be my sponsor shortly after Alton cut me loose. I admired Dick's easygoing nature and sensed that he was more of a spiritual man than he actually let on. This was what I really wanted—to become more spiritual, since I learned the hard way that all the material possessions in the world wouldn't keep you happy and content for long.

Dick and I got together one afternoon over at my house, and I explained, blow by blow, the financial nightmares I'd created for myself and why Alton told me to find another sponsor. I went on to talk about needing to learn more about humility in order to make amends to the people that I'd caused harm to, both before and after I got sober. I wanted Dick to know everything about me and that I'd do whatever was asked of me to get comfortable in my own skin and learn to live right.

After admitting my serious limitations concerning money matters, Dick suggested that I speak to Aaron D. and ask him for help. I knew Aaron from the "lunch bunch" group and the Heil Street meeting. This group was a number of men Dick had rounded up to share a lunch with on Wednesday afternoons and then go visit me at whatever hospital I was in at the time in order for me to access a meeting. When I wasn't in the hospital, I went to lunch with the guys and enjoyed their fellowship. The lunch bunch group still gets together every week to this day.

Aaron was about twenty years sober at the time, suffered from post-polio syndrome, and used a Rascal scooter to get around so that his legs wouldn't get taxed. I met with him and explained my inability to handle finances, that I had a tax-free annuity for life in addition to my social security income, and that I was tired of always screwing things up. Aaron told me that he'd be more than happy to teach me how to handle money properly, provided I did one thing: turn over all my money and bills to his control. I was startled by what I thought was a pretty extreme measure and told him that I needed to think about it first. Dick assured me that Aaron was the most honest man he knew, and he didn't have any worries because Aaron would teach me a few things. I agreed to turn over my checks and bills to Aaron every month and started to learn about budgeting. Aaron put me on an allowance, which I didn't like so much but knew it was necessary if I was going to learn about money management. Although there were numerous times when Aaron and I had heated discussions concerning my allowance, we soon became close friends.

At one point, I managed to squirrel away sixty dollars. One day, Hector and I went to a clinic to see one of my many doctors. We were told that the doctor was tied up elsewhere and wouldn't be back for couple of hours. Hector suggested that we go to a stripper bar down the street to kill some time, and I agreed. I foolishly spent the sixty dollars on lap dances, like it was going to do something for me. When Aaron found out about it, he tightened the leash on my allowance, and, of course, I didn't hear the end of it for another six months.

Although Aaron and I constantly argued about money matters, we harassed each other as only good friends can. People attending the Wednesday night meeting would laugh at the two of us drag racing in the parking lot. Aaron's scooter would edge out my wheelchair in a straight-line race. However, he couldn't pop wheelies like I could with my chair. As we got closer, I started to learn the nuances of handling finances in spite of myself.

The garage attached to Bill's condo was occupied by three motorcycles. He had two Harley Davidsons and an older BMW motorcycle. I was able to talk him through overhauling the carburetors on the BMW because they were the same kind of side-draft carbs I'd worked on for years before my accident. The experience started me thinking about possibly teaching auto shop, but I knew it would require a college degree. I began checking out what I was going to have to do.

I eventually sought help from the California Department of Rehabilitation. After my initial assessment was completed, I was warned off-the-record of the reality that although the Americans with Disabilities Act was in place, few institutions would hire a guy in a wheelchair to teach auto shop. Even though I had the actual hands-on experience, certificates and licenses that were still current, and the aptitude, as well as the passion to teach, any effort on my part to pursue this ambition would probably prove fruitless. It was suggested that I think about other alternatives as a career.

So I began to examine other options. I'd always been told that I had a "face for radio" and began to investigate various colleges in the area that offered radio broadcasting courses. I found out that Cerritos Community College offered broadcasting courses and had its own radio and TV stations. This seemed ideal because the college was nearby, so I decided to enroll for the fall semester. After taking the college entrance exams, I was pleasantly surprised to find out that because my reading was at a sixteenth-grade level, I wouldn't require any remedial courses to start. The Department of Rehabilitation committed to cover tuition and book costs, provided I stayed a full-time student.

I was concerned, however, about my age compared with the rest of the student body. One Friday night at my home group, I was expressing this to a friend, Nat M, "I'm going to be over forty when I graduate." Nat laughed and said, "John, think about it, you're going to be over forty, no matter what you do!" I laughed and told him that I'd never thought about it that way.

Chapter 12
Chipping Away at the Rough Edges

"Sought through prayer and meditation to improve our conscious contact with God, praying only for knowledge of his will for us and the power to carry it out."
(Step 11 of Alcoholics Anonymous)

In the spring of 1992, I was asked to speak at a meeting in San Luis Obispo. I asked Joyce to come with me on the trip because I'd be there for a few days. Joyce agreed to go, provided I wouldn't try any "funny stuff." I smiled and said that wouldn't be a problem, I reserved adjoining rooms at a local hotel. We left on a Thursday to enjoy a new adventure.

We met our hosts Friday morning, and they told us that they'd taken the liberty of booking a tour of Hearst Castle. They admitted not knowing how it was going to work because a bus normally took everyone up the hill to the main building. When we got there, the tour guides asked me to follow the bus in my van and park in the back lot. After reaching the top of the hill and parking, we were met by a tour guide, who gave us a private tour of the castle that included areas not normally open to the public. After the one-of-a-kind tour, we were gathered around the van preparing to leave when I made the comment, "I guess it really pays to hang out with a gimp." I immediately sensed that our hosts were uncomfortable with my remark, and I explained how I used the word "gimp" as a positive affirmation for myself. I turned it into an acronym: "Greatly Improved My Perceptions." This was something I expounded on during the talk I gave later that evening.

Usually, about five or ten minutes before speaking at a meeting, I've always developed an overwhelming urge to throw up, causing me to disappear and find a quiet place to pray. I always recite the third- and seventh-step prayers, asking God to use me as His channel to possibly help someone during the course of the evening. I once asked Frank if the impulse to throw up was normal. He told me that it was and that if I ever lost the urge, I should stop talking at meetings because my ego was taking over—and I still use this as a barometer today. I'd always return to the room as the meeting started, feeling a little bit better.

Something was different about the atmosphere, as well as the talk I gave that night. First of all, I asked everyone to stand up and give the people around them a hug, welcoming each other to the meeting. As the commotion died down, I explained how lost, lonely, afraid, and tired I was at the very first AA meeting I attended and how the hug I received that night kept me coming back for a long time before taking the twelve steps. I thanked everyone for that reminder.

I was in an unfamiliar zone as I told my story—how the application of the twelve steps had saved my life, in spite of what I thought in the beginning and the ensuing years. You could hear a pin drop in the room as I went through each of the steps, explaining how much I had learned about myself during the process, my many character defects, the qualities I discovered buried so deeply beneath the debris as I worked to clean it up, and how my attitudes started to change, although painfully so at times. For the first time, I was able to articulate the gratitude I felt at having the car accident exactly when it happened. I described how and why I had to go through all of the stuff I did in order to finally look at the world through the prism of acceptance.

I remember talking about the clarity I was striving to achieve in my "life stone," and although there were still a lot of rough edges to work on, so many of its facets had changed because I now looked at things from an entirely different point of view. I mentioned the "gimp" acronym and how being in a wheelchair coupled with the steps affected me so profoundly. I'd never shared from the podium my father's reaction; who looked at me as if I was out of my mind when I told him that I was more of a man than I'd ever been in my life, and it didn't depend on what I was wearing, what I was driving, how much money I had in the bank, or what woman was on my arm...

Being a former mechanic, I used the analogy of the Big Book as my "shop manual for life." With it I was not only able to diagnose the problem but also follow the instructions and conduct the repair work necessary to fix it. I was finally starting to grow up and become the kind of man I always wanted to be, but never knew how. I attributed a lot of the "growing up" process to the eleventh step. I had the feeling that using the third and seventh step prayers in tandem fulfilled the exact intent of the eleventh step; I no longer prayed for my own selfish ends but instead how I could help someone. I also talked about the things we take for granted until they're taken away, and how God, AA and the people close to me helped me out so much in summoning the courage to truly have a life—although it was far different from anything I ever imagined, yet infinitely more satisfying.

Before finally getting sober, I always had a vague idea in the back of my mind of the kind of man I wanted to be, but the image was so deeply shrouded in the shadows that it was unrecognizable. I learned that the vision was so out of focus because of the many years of alcohol and drug abuse and the twisted perceptions resulting from it. When the seed of willingness was planted in me and took root, it ultimately led to a journey that involved applying the steps in my life. Over time, it eventually gave my "life stone" some clarity as I chipped away at the rough edges and polished the facets, revealing a person I didn't know existed. I was becoming a man with principles and integrity that slowly rose to the surface as the character defects I had were cast aside one by one.

During the talk that night, I made a statement that eventually became one of my trademarks: "If my life gets any better, I'm going to throw up!" As I uttered those words, my face felt red as a single tear rolled down my cheek because I truly meant them. I looked down at my watch and saw that an hour and a half had passed, yet it only seemed like five minutes.

I finished the talk with a story I first heard when I was three or four months sober and didn't understand until that very evening:

There were two cats in an alley—an old cat and a little kitten… The old cat was sitting on a trashcan watching the kitten in the middle of alley running around in circles, chasing its tail. The older cat asked the kitten, "What are you doing?"
The kitten stopped—all bright-eyed and bushy-tailed, and said, "I just got back from cat philosophy school and learned that happiness is located in my tail. Don't you get it? If I chase my

tail hard enough and long enough, sooner or later I'll clamp onto it and be the happiest cat alive!"

The old cat just smiled and said, "I've been around a long time and never been to cat philosophy school, but I agree with you—happiness is located in my tail, but I do things a little differently... As long as I wake up and show up to do whatever's put in front of me, happiness follows me wherever I go.

I use this story to finish my talks to this day...

After the meeting, I was embarrassed because I'd spoken for so long. A line formed in front of me as the attendees thanked me for sharing my story and told me how much I reminded them of the work they still had to do. As Joyce and I drove back to the hotel, I secretly thanked God for allowing me to somehow be His conduit because I knew that I wasn't the only one talking during the meeting. I slept soundly that night with a quiet heart.

The next morning, our hosts invited us to spend the day at their ranch. It turned out to be a perfect day, without a cloud in the sky. Late in the afternoon, I thanked our new friends for their hospitality and told them that Joyce and I had to leave so we could get an early start back to Fullerton the next morning. As we were having dinner at the hotel, I asked Joyce if she had a "clone" sister because I would really like to go out with her. Joyce asked, "What's wrong with me?" For a moment there was an uncomfortable silence, and I explained that our relationship would be way too complicated because she worked for me. As Joyce was putting me into bed later, I felt like an idiot for asking her such a stupid question. The next morning, we packed up everything into the van for the trip home, and nothing more was said about my comment of the night before.

Sundays became what I referred to as "park days." I finally started to learn something of moderation and would stay in bed, taking a day off from my schedule. Joyce would come in the morning, give me a bed bath, change whatever dressings I had, and would set me up with a large cup of tea, including whatever reading material I wanted for the day. Usually, Bill and I would spend the day playing cribbage or just "shooting the breeze." She'd return in the late afternoon to prepare dinner for me.

One Sunday, several months after our road trip to San Luis Obispo, Joyce was getting ready to leave when out of the blue, I asked her for a kiss. After what turned out to be a long and passionate kiss, she left, saying she'd see me the next weekend. I felt as if I'd crossed the line and would probably have to start looking for a new weekend attendant. Bill and Hector both shook their heads and said that I'd better be careful if I was going to start something.

As the weekend approached, I developed a feeling of dread. My friend Bob S. says it best: "Alcoholics suffer from deeply ingrained negative thought patterns." I was surprised when Joyce came in acting as if nothing at all had happened the previous weekend. We went through the usual routine to get me ready for the rest for my day. I ran errands, hung out with friends, and went to a meeting that evening. When I finally got home, Joyce was waiting to put me into bed. Afterward, she sat on the edge of the bed and said that she really cared about me and wanted us to be involved romantically. She went on to say that she'd be willing to work for free on the weekends. After hearing this, I told her that if we were going to have a romantic relationship, there were only two options. Either I would hire another weekend attendant, or she would still be paid for the work she did, but we had to keep our professional and romantic relationships separate. We agreed to try the latter.

After several conversations with Dick and Aaron, I came to the conclusion that if college was going to work out for me, I needed to tighten the financial belt even more. I started looking for an apartment that was cheap, clean, and had a roll-in shower. I decided that if this was going to happen, the time for compromises was over.

I found a small two-bedroom apartment in Long Beach that had a roll-in shower and underground parking for the van. After going over it with Aaron, I put a deposit on the place so that I could move in the next month. I explained the situation to Bill and why I had to make the move. Although Bill said he would miss me, he thought it was a great idea, especially since Hector had decided to move in with me. I rented a truck, and my friends helped to empty out the storage facility, with the exception of my gym equipment, and moved everything else into the new apartment.

Chapter 13
A New Stage of Growth Begins

After I was settled into the new apartment, the day arrived when I attended a college class for the first time. I'd already gone to several orientation sessions and discovered that because I was a disabled student, assistance would be provided for me to take notes in my classes. I was, however, disappointed when I found out that the college radio and TV stations weren't wheelchair-accessible. On the first day of classes, it was funny that one of the other students had mistaken me for the professor teaching the course. I decided to take the broadcasting classes anyway, concentrating on taking the core curriculum required, regardless of whatever I ultimately decided to major in.

One elective class I took during the first semester was an introductory computer class, including basic overviews of computers and what they were capable of. I approached the Department of Rehabilitation after taking the course, asking if there was any assistance available to purchase a computer to help me in the writing classes I knew were coming in the future. My first computer, though it had the bells and whistles available at the time, would be stored in a museum today, but it served its purpose then.

One required course I took was an introductory political science class. I soon had such a passion for the subject that I registered as a voter for the first time in my life and participated in the 1992 presidential election that year. What a feeling to know that I was finally playing an active part in being a member of society! I eagerly went to the college administration building and switched my major to political science.

My enthusiasm for the topic spilled over into the college student body scene. I soon became a liaison and activist for the disabled student population. I also became a member of the student body, acting on many faculty committees and winning several awards for the small contributions I was able to make. There were nights when I was amazed at receiving calls at home from faculty members asking for *my* opinion on issues. I would think to myself, *This is not supposed to be happening to a hope-to-die drunk like me.*

With the help of other disabled students and a few faculty members, we eventually started a petition drive and fundraising efforts to remodel and upgrade the college radio station to make it wheelchair accessible. These efforts came to fruition when the FM radio station was gutted and remodeled a few months after I graduated making it a fully updated and accessible working classroom.

I also discovered during my college experience that I possessed a small talent and an immense love for writing. While in one of the advanced creative writing classes I took, I made a comment to the professor about what I felt was a lower grade than I deserved on a paper I'd just written, in front of the class illustrating, one more time, another one of my major character defects—arrogance. At the conclusion of the class, the professor asked me to stay behind because she wanted to talk to me. I was told in no uncertain terms that I wasn't welcome any longer in her class and that I should withdraw.

After talking to a few of my friends who worked in the Disabled Student Services Department, it was easy to conclude that I had put my foot in my mouth one more time and needed to apologize for my behavior. Thank God the tenth step is exactly where it's at. I immediately went to see the professor in her office after classes to tell her that I would withdraw from her class as she wished. I went on to admit that I was out of line and wrong in the way I behaved earlier that day. I humbly asked her if I could sign up for her class the following semester, promising a different attitude on my part. She agreed and made it clear that she was not going to cut me any slack. I took her class the following semester and received an A.

Cerritos College has a state-of-the-art automotive technology department, including programs for Ford, Chevrolet, and Chrysler technicians. As I wrestled with the desire to teach auto shop, even after learning about the negative responses I'd probably receive if I pursued the idea, I became friends with one of the Ford instructors. When he learned of my background as a former Jaguar technician, he approached the dean of the department who taught the GM courses, suggesting that I should be allowed to attend classes in spite of my disability. The dean reluctantly agreed and let me attend the initial classes. Within two weeks I was his teaching assistant and was showing the class how to do valve jobs in the machine shop. I went to the college administration building again and added automotive technology as a second major.

With Hector as my roommate, it was easier for us to become even closer friends. My routine soon consisted of going to classes, studying during breaks, going to meetings, and finally coming home to go to bed. I had Hector set up my computer on a projection cart that he would place next to my Craftmatic-style bed, since I'd do homework late into the night. I was amazed that I was able to keep a 4.0 GPA for most of my college career with the few brain cells I had left.

Once, while at a meeting, I had a realization about myself. These moments will come to us if we stick around and do this deal. Although I was attending college, I didn't have a high school diploma! My mind drifted back to my senior year in high school, when I thought I had it going on. I was the student council president in 1974 at a small school in northern Maine. I had a chance at a music scholarship at Boston University and was the school's only drug dealer as well. Shortly before graduation, a warrant was issued for my arrest. I left town in a bit of a hurry to avoid the possible consequences, ending up in Baltimore, passing myself off as a twenty-one-year-old while selling encyclopedias door to door.

Several months later, I screwed up one more time and found that I had no choice but to return to Maine and turn myself in to the police. I discovered that an adult can't be prosecuted for something they did as a minor. So I thought I got off... But did I? I lost my high school diploma and any chance at a scholarship. When I approached the school board to take my final exams, I was turned down. For the next twenty years, every time I filled out an employment application, I wrote down that I had a diploma. When I applied to the college I was attending, I honestly believed the lie I'd told everyone and myself for so many years!

Once I realized the full extent of the lie I'd been living, I knew the tenth step would come into play again as I approached the administration to tell the truth. I was almost in tears the next day while admitting everything to one of the administrators. The man chuckled a bit after I fessed up and told me that the situation happened twenty years ago and that not a lot of people knew it, but in California, you don't need a high school diploma to obtain a college degree! Today, I have two college degrees but no high school diploma.

We started a Big Book step study on Tuesday nights in the apartment, calling it the CBS (Crazy but Sober) group for the guys I sponsored, as well as the guys they sponsored. I was looking around the living room one night and saw four generations of sponsorship in the same room! We all had one goal in common, to become better men than we were the day before. Arik P., Wayne M., Dominic R., Andy H., and several others became core members of the group. We got to know more about each other, but more importantly, we learned more about ourselves.

I was paid one of the highest compliments ever when Wayne pulled me aside at the Wednesday night meeting we both attended. He told me that the first time he heard me say, "If my life gets any better, I'm going to throw up," he honestly thought that I was full of it. Wayne went on to say that after spending some time with me, he knew it was the truth, and he admired me for the man I was. For once in my life, I was speechless...

Sometime during the late spring of 1994, I was talking with Aaron when the subject of making amends to my youngest sister Linda came up. He directed me to get on the telephone and take care of it. When I called her and finished admitting all of my wrongs, Linda told me that as far as she was concerned, she no longer had a brother, and I should never contact her again. As I put down the phone, the tears of sorrow soon turned to anger as I called Aaron to tell him what happened. Aaron calmly referred me to the section of the Big Book, where it states: "It should not matter, however, if someone does throw us out of his office. We have made our demonstration, done our part," (page 78) He reminded me that it's not important if our amends are accepted or not—as long as we don't bring about more harm to the person we are making them to. Aaron suggested that I respect my sister's wishes and leave her alone. That was the price I was going to have to pay.

After rereading the part of the Big Book specific to steps eight and nine (pages 76–85), I accepted what he told me and came to the conclusion that if my "life stone" was going to become truly transparent, I had to believe in the process, no matter what personal demons or emotional pains I had to overcome or live with. I conceded that although I'd come a long way in my personal program of recovery, I still had such a long way to go.

Every five years, an International Convention is hosted by Alcoholics Anonymous somewhere in North America. In the summer of 1995, it was held in San Diego, only a two-hour drive from where I was living. I volunteered to be a part of the Special Needs Committee and made the trip to San Diego several times during the year leading up to the event. On one occasion, I was on the field at what was then called Jack Murphy Stadium, in awe of its size from my vantage point, and I tried to imagine what it would be like filled with a bunch of sober drunks. It took everything in me not to take the wheelchair around the bases, since the field was pristine awaiting a Padres game that night.

I had tickets as well as hotel accommodations for the convention, and Joyce was going to accompany me. A week out from the event, she told me that she couldn't make it because of a family situation. After checking with Hector and everyone else I knew that could function as my attendant, it was apparent that I wouldn't be able to attend the convention. I decided to give my tickets and room to a couple of guys I sponsored because I knew they couldn't afford to go otherwise. On Friday night, the beginning of the convention, I was in bed watching television when I got a call from Ken S., one of the men I sponsored. He was calling on his cell phone from Jack Murphy Stadium. I heard friends yelling their hellos and also heard the opening ceremony as if I were actually there! I started crying so hard that eventually the buttons shorted out on the cordless phone I was using, and I couldn't call anyone until the next morning after everything dried out.

Note: Later that evening, Ken was in a bar wearing his AA nametag, getting drunk... This was an "in-my-face" reminder for me that no one is cured once he or she gets sober. I was told later about a man who had forty-two years of continuous sobriety. He got a bright idea one day, and they found him in his apartment two weeks later, dead from alcohol poisoning. It was like a billboard sign for me when I overheard an old-timer say to another, "The guy had too many years—and not enough days." I've been counting my days ever since…

The following Friday night, I was headed to my home group in La Palma and made my usual pit stop at a coffee shop two blocks from the meeting. After paying for the coffee, I started toward the exit when the clerk came from behind the counter to hold the door open for me. As I crossed the threshold, one of the front wheels on my wheelchair snapped off! The coffee went flying as I tottered and almost fell over on my head, had it not been for the quick reflexes of the coffee shop employee. He helped me guide the chair to a pole to lean against while I used my cell phone to call my buddy Bob S., who was already at the meeting. Bob hopped into his truck to come to the rescue. He helped me enter and lock down in the van and followed me to the meeting, balancing the chair for me as we made our way into the building. Once I found a place to park at one of the tables, Bob grabbed three Big Books to put under my chair, where the wheel used to be. We discovered another of the plethora of uses for the book, aside from being a coaster or doorstop! The best use, of course, is to read it and apply what's between the covers to save an alcoholic's life…

Chapter 14
Emotional Sobriety, Finding Humor in Adversity, and Making a Contribution

After taking a couple of elective courses during the summer, I started the fall semester optimistic about graduation and the somewhat remote possibility of starting a teaching career. I was increasingly distracted, however, from the daily routine every time I examined my eighth-step list. A name at the top of the list was causing an emotional knot in the pit of my stomach—Kandy, the woman who had moved to California with me.

One Wednesday afternoon, after having a meal with the lunch bunch group, I asked Dick for a few minutes of his time to explain the quandary I was in. I'd tried over the years to track her down by calling 411 in the Cleveland area. I had also looked for her relatives, but it was like the entire family fell off the face of the Earth. I went on to tell Dick that the amends I needed to make was beginning to be a burden on my soul and that I was having a hard time living with it because of the depth of harm I'd caused. Dick suggested that I write her an amends letter as if I had an address to send it to. It took me all night to write it because it was as if I were reliving our relationship from the first time we met, and I saw everything clearly through a window—looking at a man I could only feel pity for because "he didn't know that he didn't know…"

A few days later, I read the letter to Dick from beginning to end with tears streaming down my face because I was so ashamed of the things I did. This woman, who had always believed in and stood up for me, certainly didn't deserve the emotional pain I'd inflicted on her. When I was done, he told me to keep the letter on my computer because the day might come when I'd have the opportunity to make a face-to-face amends to her. I agreed, and the load I was carrying lessoned a bit.

Late one evening, while I was doing homework on my computer, I received a phone call from my sister, Linda. She told me that although she'd probably never forgive me for the things I'd done in the past, my nephew and niece needed to have their Uncle John in their life. Linda asked me to visit Texas and spend Christmas with them and our brother Bob, who was stationed at an army base an hour away from her. I accepted her invitation and was stunned as I hung up.

I brought up the idea of taking a road trip during Christmas break to Joyce, who excitedly suggested that while there I should meet her parents, since they lived in Arkansas, just a few miles from the Texas border. We proceeded to make plans for a December adventure. This wasn't much different from the journey we had taken the previous year to visit my friend Nat in Cottonwood, Arizona to spend Thanksgiving with him and his family.

After doing a search on the Internet, I found that the best place to stay was near Ft. Hood, where Bob was stationed, since I could not find any hotels that were fully accessible with a roll-in shower. The holiday break from school arrived. Hector helped us load the van, and we were off.

We arrived in Texas a day early to get some much-needed rest after the long drive. The next morning, Joyce mentioned that there was a minor red blemish on my butt. I had just purchased a collapsible shower chair made for traveling that could possibly be the cause. I made a mental note to look at the cheek later that evening.

Bob showed up at the door to lead the way to his house off-post, and I introduced him to Joyce. He'd taken the time to build a sturdy ramp for me to get into the house. We had coffee and caught up on things when Linda, her husband, and their kids, Christina and J.J., arrived, completing our reunion. While everyone was talking and laughing, Linda and I had a moment alone when I was able to tell her how much it meant for me to be there. She said it was great and that we should make the most of it and have a good time.

We really enjoyed the next couple of days celebrating the Christmas holiday. Bob had a second career as a photographer and took pictures every chance he got. I was secretly thanking God that the pictures he was taking of me were not like the collection my parents had of holiday snapshots when I was usually in a drunken stupor. He and I had an afternoon to ourselves when we made a trip to San Antonio to check out the Alamo. I took the opportunity to make amends to my brother and thank him for saving my life when I was in the ICU after the car accident.

The day after Christmas, we said good-bye to everyone and left for Boston, Texas, to visit Joyce's family. When we got there and settled into the hotel room, Joyce grabbed a hand mirror so that I could look at my butt. The blemish had started to turn into a larger, angry-looking red area. I told her that we needed to severely restrict my time sitting on the shower chair because there was something definitely wrong with the cushion.

The next morning as we were driving into Arkansas, I expressed apprehension about what Joyce's parents might think about the idea of her dating a white guy (Joyce is African-American). She confided to me that it wasn't really a big deal because they already knew everything. Joyce's brothers were there to meet us and had put together a makeshift ramp for me to enter the small, cozy home to meet the rest of the family. I felt welcome as she introduced me to her family, and we had an awesome dinner. As we were leaving to return to the hotel, I thanked them all for their hospitality.

I examined my rear end that night, and I knew I was in trouble. The spot had grown to the size of my fist, and the redness was surrounded by light purple, looking like a bruise. I made a decision to stay in bed for a couple of days to try to clear up the wound. I lost consciousness the next day...

I came to in a hospital room with Joyce at my side. When the doctor came into the room, I was told the harsh truth—the affected area on my buttocks was now all dead tissue, and the infection had become septic; in other words, it had gone into my bloodstream. If Joyce had waited even a couple of hours before calling 911, chances were that I'd be dead. The doctor told me that he'd already talked to my insurance company, and they wanted him to get me stabilized well enough to transport home. I started making arrangements to get my van and things back to California. I called Hector, asking him to take care of it for me, so I booked a flight for him to come and get the van.

The next day, Joyce and I rode in an ambulance to the local airport, and I was surprised to find out that my medical insurance covered the cost of the chartered jet to make the trip. Once we landed at Long Beach Airport, another ambulance ride took us to the hospital, where I was immediately prepped for surgery. There is an old saying in AA meetings: "Go to a meeting no matter what—even if your ass falls off—if it does, put it in a brown paper bag and take it with you..." I was trying to keep a sense of humor when I asked the surgeon to put what he was going to remove from my rear end in a bag for me, and of course, the doctor looked at me as if I had lost my mind.

In the recovery room after the surgery, the doctor working on my wound explained that there was so much dead tissue to be cut away that he couldn't stitch the site closed. He said that over time, using a specific course of treatment, the wound would fill in on its own and eventually heal. I knew my body well enough to know that the healing process would take months, possibly even years.

Realizing the full impact of the situation, I called the college to withdraw from the classes that I had signed up for. I was pleased to find out that there were a few extra courses I could take online. So when I was eventually transferred to a convalescent hospital, I asked for and received permission to have a temporary telephone line installed for my computer so we could set it up in my room. For the next three months I was able to continue taking college courses while the slow process of healing continued.

Every Wednesday, the lunch bunch group would come to see me and have a meeting in the hospital room. I also joined an online men's group to help keep my sanity as the days moved on slowly at a snail's pace. I concentrated on doing my homework and writing while playing soft music on the computer because it was soothing and helped with my creativity and my focus on the paper I was doing.

I was fortunate that the huge wound was high on my backside. When it was more than halfway "filled in," I could finally get into my power wheelchair without causing any more damage. I was discharged with instructions not to overdo it, and I concentrated on finishing my college education.

After I came home to the small apartment, Buzz called me one afternoon asking for help with installing a computer in his shop, setting up the necessary programs, and teaching him how to use it. I enthusiastically set it up for my friend. I was able to enter a complete parts menu with prices that he used, as well as labor costs for every type of repair he did. It was a tedious process to teach Buzz how to use it and streamline his business. He learned that the software would allow him to generate a monthly profit and loss statement, as well as reminders to mail to his customers when the time came for regular maintenance. Buzz asked me if I would consider being the service manager on Saturdays for him now that everything was computerized. I could use the extra cash, so I agreed.

The spring turned out to be an extremely busy one because I was back at college full-time, working for Buzz on Saturdays, and going to five meetings a week. By this point, Aaron felt I'd learned enough from him about handling money properly, so, after giving me a few strategies to restore my credit rating, he relinquished control of my finances back to me. My relationships with the people close to me were better than ever because I was showing up and finally growing up. It began to feel as if my "life stone" started to become more transparent as time went on, and I was becoming the type of man I sensed that God wanted me to be. All of the footwork I'd done up to that point in my life still didn't prepare me for the series of events that would come out of left field throughout the upcoming summer…

One afternoon, I went over to Aaron's house to give him a lift to a doctor's appointment and to meet his eighty-five-year-old mother, who was in town visiting him. After being introduced to his mother, I noticed that Aaron didn't seem to be his usual self. He seemed lethargic, and although he was wearing an oxygen line, my friend's lips were blue. I immediately grabbed the phone and called 911, despite his objections. The ambulance came and took him to the hospital. His mother rode with Aaron, and I told her that I'd meet her in the waiting room.

I spent the entire afternoon with Aaron's mom as we waited for a doctor to tell us how he was. An intern finally came out to let us know that Aaron was stable and was suffering from oxygen deprivation. Although his post-polio syndrome was getting worse, he'd be well enough to go home in a few days. Aaron's mother gave me a hug and thanked me for being so insistent on calling the EMTs. I spent the next few days with her, comforting her as best I could until he was well enough to go home. As Aaron was being loaded into the ambulance, I made my way to the van with tears streaming down my cheeks as I reflected on the large number of unknown members of AA who supported my parents when I was at the precipice between life and death. Things, in a small way, had come full circle, and I thanked God that I was put at the right place at the right time.

Chapter 15
Planting Seeds, Still Learning, and Being of Service

"Having had a spiritual awakening as the result of these steps, we tried to carry this message to alcoholics, and to practice these principles in all our affairs."
(Step 12 of Alcoholics Anonymous)

One of the benefits of my early experiences with the long-timers I met in AA was the training I received concerning the necessity of 12-Step work. My first sponsor was heavily involved with the local H&I committee and introduced me to other men and women making the same efforts. They soon started dragging me all over southern California, going to hospitals, institutions, rehab centers, and the like to bring meetings to those who couldn't get to ones on the outside. Although I understood the basic concept that helping another drunk would help me stay sober, I didn't think then that I had anything to offer.

I started to get a clue after my first road trip with Buck. We went to a place called the Cider House, a halfway house for men coming out of treatment or jail who didn't have anywhere to go. After the meeting, Buck stepped back into a corner and watched. Some of the guys came to me asking how I was able to stay sober for the three or four months I had at the time. On the way home, Buck explained to me that newly sober people usually can't relate to someone who has multiple years of sobriety but are almost always interested in a person who's been sober for even a few months. (I always bring new guys I'm working with to the institutions and detox centers I visit to this day and do the same thing.)

Another road trip involved a four-hour drive to a penitentiary out in the middle of the desert. After the meeting, they started driving back, and I didn't understand why these guys did this regularly at their own expense. I asked the old-timer sitting next to me, "What do you guys get out of this?" Before exposure to AA, my world was one where you never did anything for anyone unless there was something in it for you—I even thought that when they passed the basket at my first meeting, it was to pay for Bill H.'s expenses!

The man sitting next to me turned, smiled, and said one of those old timer-isms: "When you do what we do, you'll see what we get." A few years after the accident, I was driving the van to the same penitentiary when a newcomer asked me what I got out of going to this out-of-the way place. Guess what my response was...

After years of performing 12-Step work on a regular basis, two things became apparent to me:

1. The message referred to in step twelve is real simple—if a person diligently takes the previous eleven steps, they will have a spiritual awakening... In other words, a person *can* change in spite of themselves.
2. Although I knew it was necessary to do this "12-Step stuff" to save my own skin, during early sobriety doing it grudgingly because it was against my normal nature—a transition occurred before I realized it—saving my skin grew to be secondary. The motivating factor became purely the joy of it. Nothing on this Earth gives me more gratification than seeing a person's lights come on!

Every other Tuesday, I used to bring a meeting to the Metropolitan State Hospital in Norwalk. I would go in to the "lockdown" psych unit at 11:00 a.m., usually before the patients received their meds. One morning, in early 1991 during the first Gulf War, I got off the elevator and was greeted by Dave, one of the patients who would probably never leave the unit because of his mental illness. Dave was dressed in crisply ironed khakis and was wearing a green tie. When I asked about his outfit, Dave replied, "John, haven't you heard?" I asked him what he was talking about, and he answered, "There's a war going on, and I might be called because they're going to need paratroopers!" I smiled inwardly at my friend's delusion as we made our way to the meeting room. During the meeting, Dave's demeanor changed, and he seemed to be a different person entirely as he accepted a coin for nine years of sobriety. There is a line in the beginning of Chapter Five of the Big Book that states: "There are those, too, who suffer from grave emotional and mental disorders, but many of them do recover if they have the capacity to be honest." (page 58) Dave was the perfect example of this truism.

A few years later, I was giving a talk at a meeting at HOW Hall, an Alano Club in the Huntington Beach area. I was approached by a young man after the meeting. He asked if I remembered him, and when I told him that I didn't, he said, "You spoke at Martin Luther King Hospital about three years ago when I was in treatment. A lot of the things you said were so profound that they've stuck with me ever since, and I just wanted to thank you for that..." I asked him how long he was sober and was surprised to find out that he had thirty days of sobriety.

I had another epiphany as a result of that experience when it comes to 12-Step work—I concluded that I'm only in the "seed-planting" business. It's up to God when and if the seeds are going to take root or not. Learning how to look at things from a different perspective not only taught me how to have compassion, empathy, and listening skills, but it has allowed me to get out of myself for the newly sober person. These attributes eventually became part of my toolbox to help me spread the message of hope, or, if you will, "plant the seeds." When I first started to sponsor guys, I would take it personally when a man couldn't or wouldn't adopt the principles outlined in the Big Book and go get loaded again. What a freedom it was to *know* that all I could do was just be an example and let God be in charge of the rest...

This sudden intuitive leap of understanding had an effect in other areas of my life as well. In the spring of 1996, after I'd been discharged from the convalescent hospital, I was on campus soaking up rays and studying one of my textbooks between classes when I was approached by one of the students. The young man inquired, "Excuse me, sir, I just wanted to ask do you know Jesus Christ?"

"Not personally, do you?" I replied. The student went on to explain that he did indeed and wanted to pray with me for the ability to walk again. Without blinking, I explained to the young man that I had my own relationship with a God of my understanding, was perfectly okay with my circumstance, and had no desire to walk again but thanked him nonetheless. The student left with a stunned look as I reflected on another story

I'd heard early in sobriety that didn't make sense to me at the time:

A group of drunks were playing a five-card poker game, and God was dealing the cards. When they got their first draw, they started complaining about the rotten cards they had. Each player at the table threw in three cards for the final draw. The players examined their cards and mumbled under their breath things like, "I don't deserve such a rotten hand like this," and "If you had cards like this, you'd be a drunk and loser too..." After a time, God leaned over to look at each player in the eye and asked, "Why can't you knuckleheads just be happy you're in the game?"

    I took a deep breath, understanding with absolute clarity that I was perfectly content with the hand of cards dealt to me. Despite the numerous physical, emotional, and spiritual pitfalls I'd encountered during my life, they were *my* cards, and I wouldn't trade them for all the tea in China. All too often, I went to discussion meetings leaving with a sense of gratitude that I had my own problems to deal with and not anyone else's because I wasn't sure I'd cope with them if put in their position. It's like the analogy of a person having a hangnail and another having a broken leg... Both are painful, and who can be sure that they would trade places if each *really* knew how much pain the other was suffering?

    Late in the evening on June 24, 1996 (the ninth anniversary of my accident), I took a break from an assignment I was working on and started to surf the Internet. I came across a search engine that was used to look for people using telephone books throughout the country. Kandy's name came to my mind immediately, and I thought, *What the heck, I've tried everything else.* I typed in her name and clicked on the go button... I thought about the various times throughout the years when I was convinced I'd seen her out of the corner of my eye while driving down Beach Boulevard or some other street and immediately turned around, only to be disappointed at finding out it wasn't her after all. My attention returned to the computer screen as it changed, showing her name, address, and telephone number. She still had her last name because she had never married. I stared at the screen in shock and disbelief into the wee hours of the morning...

The next morning, I called Dick and told him about my discovery. He reminded me of the amends letter I'd written nine months earlier and suggested that I send it to Kandy, using the address I found, certified mail with a return receipt requested. I printed and addressed the letter immediately, going to the post office to mail it.

It wasn't until the next day that I was able to find the courage to call the phone number that was blinking on my computer screen the night before. I expected to be admonished for the terrible ways I behaved years ago and was relieved to hear the answering machine come on. I listened to a voice I hadn't heard in seventeen years. I almost forgot to leave a message at the beep but managed to say something that I hoped was coherent, along with my phone number.

The letter came back to me two weeks later labeled as "undeliverable." After talking to Dick and mentioning that I hadn't received a call from her either, he agreed with my idea that maybe she didn't want to have anything to do with me after all. Dick told me, "You've done everything you can, so it's time to move on."

Buzz, in the meantime, decided to take a long-overdue extended vacation with his family to visit his mother in South Africa again and asked me to run his shop for him while he was gone. I told him I was only taking a couple of evening classes, so I'd be able to do it without a problem. He was working on only Hondas and Acuras at that point, so I had to spend a few days at the shop during the week, getting familiar with his vendors and suppliers. He made it clear to me that although I'd done an excellent job of running his shop years earlier, I wouldn't have access to the company's checking account this time. Buzz made arrangements with all of the vendors and left payroll checks for me and the rest of the staff covering the six weeks he'd be gone, as well as a few extra signed checks to be used only for unforeseen circumstances. Any bonuses due the mechanics would be taken care of upon his return.

As I familiarized myself with Buzz's shop operations, I updated the computer to reflect the latest customer data and pricing information. Buzz introduced me to the two technicians working for him, Kevin and Donny. He confided in me that Kevin, who was from New Zealand, was a "madman," just like I used to be—in that he was as fast and efficient working on Japanese cars as I'd been with British cars. Kevin could handle anything that came into the shop, whereas Donny was adept at handling regular maintenance issues. With this knowledge, I started to form a plan of action to use when Buzz left for his trip.

After coming home from the meeting in Huntington Beach one Wednesday night, my jaw dropped in disbelief as I checked my voicemail—Kandy had called me. I had left the message for her three weeks earlier and never expected a return call.

The next day, with some hesitation, I called her number and got a live voice this time. Our conversation lasted over an hour as we caught up on where our lives had taken us. After living in Cincinnati and Columbus for a period of time, dating a man for eight years and not having it work out, she decided to move back to the Cleveland area to be close to her family again. She was working for a company that specialized in software for the hospitality industry, requiring her to travel extensively, installing the hardware and software, and training hotel staff to use it.

I told her briefly how I'd married Monica about a year after she moved back to Cleveland, but six and a half years later we divorced. I also told her about the car accident, my membership in AA, going to college, and that I'd been dating Joyce for about three years. When I mentioned the amends letter that was returned, Kandy told me that she was in San Diego doing an install at the time, She remarked how glad she was that I was finally sober. (Why is it that that the alcoholic is always the last one to know that they've got a problem?) I said that I'd like to send it again because it was important to me, and she agreed to do nothing until she read the letter.

After printing and re-mailing the letter, I confided in Dick a couple of long-held secrets that I'd never openly talked about. First, I *knew* in my heart that I would see Kandy again one day, but I'd expected that she would be married, with children in tow. Secondly, after she left California seventeen years earlier, not a week had gone by without me having a passing thought about her...

Kandy accepted my amends after reading my letter. We began exchanging letters that included current pictures of each other.

Wanting to be up-front with Joyce, I told her about the amends I made and the relationship I used to have with Kandy. I even let her read the letter before I sent it the first time. I made a promise to myself when I first got sober that if I were ever in a long-term relationship again, I wouldn't ever venture outside the boundaries of it.

Chapter 16
Is John Losing His Mind?

The Saturday before Buzz was supposed to leave on his trip, I went into work as usual and was mildly surprised to see him there. He went over a few things with me, showed me the uniforms he had ordered for my use, and told me to "behave myself" while he was gone. I went home later that afternoon grateful that my buddy still trusted me enough to let me run his business while he was gone.

The first couple of weeks went as I expected. After learning of Kevin's ability for doing repair jobs so efficiently, I booked in work that kept everyone extremely busy. I was even able to help Donny with a couple of electrical problems that he had difficulty with. Despite the heavy workload, we did find time to have a good laugh or two.

One afternoon I was outside in the parking lot talking to one of the guys from a neighboring repair facility when I heard the phone ring in the shop. I put the wheelchair into high gear and raced into the garage to answer it. I sped across the enameled floor and tried to execute a ninety-degree turn to get the phone as I hit a puddle of water. It was as if everything was in slow motion when my chair slid across the shop floor sideways and slammed into the back wall so hard that the chair came up on two wheels and my head collided with the sheetrock, jarring my molars.

Through tears of laughter and the howling of everyone else in the shop, I was able to answer the phone, only to find out that it was a wrong number, which only added to the hilarity of the situation. Another day, Kevin was jokingly chasing me around the shop, waving a wrench. He had so much work on his hands that he was threatening to unplug my chair in an area where I couldn't reach the phone so nothing more could be booked.

Late one night, after a hard day at work, I got a call from Kandy telling me that she would be doing an installation job at a hotel in Costa Mesa the following week. She asked if we could have dinner together Monday night after we both got off work. I timidly agreed, and she gave me the address of the hotel she'd be at so I could pick her up. As I put the phone down, my mind was racing a mile a minute, reliving events that happened so long ago... The demons that I thought were finally put to rest came back to me in an onslaught of guilt, remorse, and, surprisingly enough—fear gripped me for the first time in years.

The next morning I called Aaron to tell him about the phone call and the upcoming dinner plans for Monday night. Aaron simply asked me, "So what's the big deal?" Before I could think about it, I confessed that I was scared to death that I would fall in love with Kandy again and get my heart broken. Aaron chuckled and told me not to project things that might or might not happen and to try to stay in the "now," making the best of it.

That weekend I told Joyce about Kandy being in town on business and our dinner plans and invited her to come along. Joyce laughed and said, "John, you're the smartest guy I know, but you're really stupid when it comes to women. There is no way I'm going, but you go and have a good time."

Monday morning arrived, and I was at the shop as Kevin arrived on his motorcycle. He unlocked the gate, and we entered the compound to get ready for business. The day flew by because I was on the phone all day, either rounding up parts for the guys or booking appointments, so I didn't have a chance to dwell on the nonsense that had gone on between my ears over the weekend. At the end of the day, the shop was "buttoned up" as I reflected on how quickly things went and how I was "in the moment" throughout our hectic schedule.

As I drove to the hotel where Kandy was working, I discovered that it was less than a mile from the apartment complex where we had lived together. I parked the van in front of the hotel and discreetly entered it, going across the lobby as far away from the front desk as I could while trying to slow down my heart, which felt as if it were going to explode from my chest. From my vantage point I was able to check out the people at the front desk, not recognizing anyone. After five or ten minutes, a door behind the check-in location opened, and there she was—even more beautiful than I remembered. I eyed her every move for some time as she interacted with the staff. I was enthralled by the obvious air of self-confidence and professionalism she exhibited, which only added to her attractiveness. As I moved to the center of the lobby, Kandy glanced up from what she was doing, and my gaze locked on to her green eyes. I felt as if I was going to melt. She raised her index figure, signaling she would be done in a minute.

She came from behind the desk, and as she approached me, I felt extremely awkward and uncomfortable. Kandy broke the ice by asking me if it was okay to give me a hug, and I could only nod. As I held her, I smelled the same perfume she wore when we were together years earlier. She told me that she needed to change before we went to dinner and asked if I wouldn't mind walking her to her room, which was on the far side of the property in another wing. As we made our way into the hotel wing, I made a mental note about the disabled parking spot next to the entrance. It only took a few minutes for Kandy to change as I waited, and we started back to the front of the hotel, where I was parked. As we walked together, I mentioned how odd it was that the apartment we used to live in was just down the street. She giggled and placed her hand on my shoulder. Inwardly, I flinched as if a thousand volts of electricity flowed through my body, but I showed no outward signs of the shock.

Arriving at the van, I showed her all the bells and whistles it had—the remote-controlled door and ramp, the hand control driving system, and, of course, my pride and joy, the thousand-watt stereo that was like a sound studio on wheels. We drove by our old apartment before going to dinner. We stared at the second-floor balcony with memories flooding our minds, some good and some bad, without saying much as we drove to the Mexican restaurant I'd chosen for dinner. We ate and talked for hours about how the events in our lives had taken us to the moment we were in now. I told her that I'd invited Joyce to join us for dinner, and Joyce's remark afterward. Kandy agreed that it was a real dumb move on my part.

The meal ended too soon, as far as I was concerned, but I paid the check and drove us back to the hotel, parking in the spot I noted earlier, to escort Kandy to her room. When we got there, she asked me if I'd like to come in for a bit. I gracefully declined (although I really didn't want to) because I had to work early the next morning and I should go home. She asked me if it would be okay if she kissed me. When we kissed, something happened to me that I've never had the words to adequately explain. It was almost as if a "zapping" had hit my pointed head, coursing through my body and making my paralyzed toes curl. There were feelings I couldn't articulate welling up from some far-reaching untouched area of my heart, and I kept telling myself it was only a figment of my imagination...

The drive to the modest little apartment in Long Beach seemed to take forever. Hector was waiting to put me to bed, and when I briefly told him about the evening, he could only shake his head and say, "You'd better be careful, Pepe; you could be getting into something you can't handle..."

After I got settled for the night, Joyce called to ask about how the dinner date went with Kandy. I told her about the evening and how we talked for hours at the restaurant. She asked if I kissed her when I left—which I readily admitted to. I wanted to be honest with her although I fell short of that because I didn't mention the dialogue going on in my head.

For the next three days I had work, school, and meetings to keep me occupied. I called Kandy at work every day and made the time to drop by the hotel to talk to her for a bit before going to class or a meeting.

I arrived early Wednesday night at the Huntington Beach meeting to tell Dick and Aaron about seeing Kandy again and what I referred to as the "silly nonsense" that was getting increasingly louder and more coherent in my thoughts. I told them about the imaginary lightning bolt that coursed through my body when she touched my shoulder and how it felt so familiar and comfortable when we kissed for the first time. I told my two mentors that I was probably deluding myself because I'd started to "fall in love with the idea of being in love" with her. I felt bad that I couldn't share this with Joyce, knowing what pain it would cause her for; after all, we'd been together three years, and I'd always told her the truth about everything.

Dick and Aaron smiled at each other and reminded me that we're not responsible for the thoughts that go through our minds but what happens if we act on them with selfish and inconsiderate actions. That's why implementing the steps in our lives work so well in filtering our actions, since people judge us by our outward behavior. I agreed with them but also stated that if a "normal" person spent five minutes in my head at any given time during the week, he'd probably have me committed. They asked me if I'd done anything that was wrong or out of line in respect to my relationship with Joyce. I thought about it and admitted that I had nothing to feel guilty or ashamed of because I'd been completely above board with regard to my behavior. The two suggested that I "stay in the moment" and try not to pay attention to what my mind might be projecting about what might or might not be happening to me.

As the week came to a close, I asked Kandy to have dinner with me on Friday night at a place I knew in Laguna Beach. I met Hector at the apartment after work to get out of my uniform and into something more suitable. I picked her up at the hotel as the sun was starting to set. The restaurant we went to was on top of a cliff overlooking the Pacific Ocean. We enjoyed an excellent dinner filled with a kind of comfortable conversation as if the seventeen years of being apart had never occurred. Afterward, we wandered out to the garden area that had sidewalks running parallel to the cliffs, lined with park benches to sit on and enjoy the sounds of the ocean waves caressing the beaches below.

Kandy sat on one of the benches, and I excused myself for a moment and went down the sidewalk to find a secluded spot where I could discreetly drain my leg bag behind a bush. When I returned, she asked if everything was okay, and I awkwardly told her what I was doing because there wasn't a handicapped-accessible bathroom in the restaurant. She told me that she was starting to get an idea of some of the things I had to deal with on a daily basis, and she was impressed. I said that there was no need for that because I was just like anyone else in this world, doing the best they could with what they had.

As we talked, the conversation began to take on more serious overtones as we went into detail about the paths our lives took over the years that we'd just glossed over before. She told me about living in southern Ohio, being involved in a long-term relationship with a man, and how it ended so badly. She mentioned a man who became her mentor as she learned about her new career in the hospitality field. Eventually, she found herself at a hotel in Clearwater, Florida, missing her family desperately. She finally got an opportunity to work for the company she was currently at, and because she traveled so much, it didn't matter where she lived, so she relocated to the

Cleveland area to be closer to her family. Although she was where she wanted to be and had the love of her family close at hand, as well as the chance to travel the world, there were times when she would be alone in her apartment between trips with all of her "stuff" and cry her eyes out because she was so lonely.

Her blunt honesty caused me to share something I'd held in my heart for so many years—*knowing* that I would see her again someday and that she'd probably be dragging a horde of kids with her in some shopping mall someplace, which caused her to giggle a bit and lightened the mood. I went on to tell her that even though I had a full life beyond anything I could've ever expected, I still felt that somehow it fell short of what it could be.

Kandy suggested that I'd made so many concessions since the accident, I was content with just settling for the status quo. I knew she was right the very instant she said those words. Tears started to flow as I told her about the things I did for AA, the people I helped both in and out of the rooms, and how I constantly had personal struggles with demons telling me I was still worthless—that I didn't deserve anything good in life because I was such a loser to begin with. Although I had a life that included purpose, friends, respect, a home, school, a job, and a girlfriend, I still had the feeling there was something very important missing. I dried my teary eyes, suggesting we leave because I wanted to show her a spot I had discovered that helped me to just chill out and enjoy the moment.

It was a cul-de-sac off the highway that went into a small cluster of homes on a cliff. I parked the van and led Kandy up a winding sidewalk that stopped at a gazebo overlooking Laguna Beach. We could see the city lights, the waves lapping on the beach, and hear the sea lions off in the distance. Amid the quiet sounds of the surf, sea lions, and the scent of the ocean, she sat in my lap and we kissed for what seemed an eternity… When our lips parted, we were both a little flustered at the intimacy we'd just shared, so we went silently to the van to go back to Kandy's hotel. When we reached her hotel room, I started to apologize when she merely put her finger on my lips to shut me up and kissed me goodnight…

As I drove home, I reviewed the entire week in my mind. I was second-guessing myself again, wondering what was really happening here. Was I losing my mind? Were the feelings I felt coming from a place deep within my heart when I was with this woman a figment of my romantic imagination? Were the vibes I felt coming from her the "real deal"? As Hector was getting me ready for bed, I told him about the time I spent with Kandy. He told me that I was really knee-deep in it this time.

The next morning, as Joyce was getting me ready to go to work, I told her that I was going to meet Kandy for lunch because she was leaving town the next day. When asked about our movie date, I told Joyce that it wouldn't be a problem meeting her because we had already planned to see the late afternoon show.

I met Kevin at the compound's gate as usual and got ready for the day's work. The morning went by quickly, and as we were locking up, I told Kevin that Kandy was leaving the next day and that I was going to meet her for lunch. I was a little startled as Kevin said, "Good, now maybe you'll get back to normal and stop acting like the silly buggar you've been all week!"

I arrived at the hotel and knocked on Kandy's door, surprised that lunch was on the table in the room. She'd ordered Chinese food, thinking it was better than spending the time going out. I sheepishly asked her if she'd mind helping me use her bathroom because I was in such a hurry that I'd forgotten to drain my leg bag. She acted as if it were a normal thing as I tilted the wheelchair back and moved it over the toilet, telling her how to open and close the drain valve. I thanked her profusely as we started having lunch.

The conversation was mostly small talk, since I was still pretty troubled about the night before. We talked about her next assignment and my plans after graduating from college. After lunch, I was sitting in the middle of the room, wondering how I was going to be able to say good-bye to this woman that had stirred my heart so... I glanced at the clock on the wall and saw that it was time for me to leave. As I kissed Kandy good-bye and wished her a good flight home, my cheeks were flushed and almost burning from an overload of feeling and emotion that I couldn't find the words to express. Before I left, I promised to call her. I backed into the van and saw a tear-filled face looking back at me in the rearview mirror.

While driving to the movie theater to meet Joyce, I was trying hard to suck it up and pull myself together emotionally. Although we didn't have sex, I knew that I'd crossed a "mental" line I promised myself years earlier never to approach again. My feelings of guilt were magnified by the imagined scent of Kandy's body on me.

I met Joyce at the theater, and she, of course, asked how lunch went with Kandy. I told her that we had Chinese food and said our good-byes. I was really grateful, since we sat in the dark theater, that the movie we were watching had quite a few sad scenes. It wasn't uncommon for me to shed tears when watching a dramatic and touching film, and several times a single tear rolled down my cheek while reflecting on the dilemma I found myself in...

It was a usual routine when Joyce and I came home from a night out that I would turn on the speakerphone in the living room and listen for messages. Without even thinking, I put on the headphone, listened, and found no messages. Joyce was strangely quiet as we got me ready for bed. The next morning after breakfast she mentioned my break from routine the night before and asked if I had something to hide. Before I could say anything, Joyce told me that she could see from the look on my face that our relationship was over—she was leaving, and I'd better find a new attendant for the weekends.

Hector was home when she left and came into my room to see if I was okay. He found me sitting up in bed in stunned silence. "Well, you really messed up this time, Pepe. What are you going to do now?" he queried. I looked at my pal and answered in a quivering voice, "I have no idea, dude."

Chapter 17
Life-Changing Decisions and Lifelong Insights

Later that afternoon, I called Kandy and quietly told her how and why Joyce left that morning. She listened silently as I described the one-sided conversations that went on between my ears throughout the week we spent together. I explained how after I left her Saturday afternoon, my heart ached because I knew the feelings I had were real and that I'd probably never see her again. "What makes you think you'll never see me again?" Kandy asked. I later learned that she thought she'd never hear from me again either and was surprised at my call. I told her that because we lived in different states, it would not only be impractical but extremely difficult for us to see each other. She made it clear that, because of the type of work she did, she could fly in or out of any area she wanted to and that she also had tons of frequent flyer miles to use as well.

I pointed out that she'd only seen me during the week, while I was already up and running around, and suggested that she spend a week or two with me to really have an up-close and personal look at what she was getting into if we were going to have a relationship of any kind. Out of the blue, Kandy said that she had some time off coming and that she could be there in a week or two.

The next day at work, I was focused with a renewed energy on what I was doing. By the middle of the week Kevin was saying, "Bloody hell, John, I wanted you to get back to normal, but not to swamp me in work again, you idiot!" But all was well, and Buzz was pleased when he called to check up on the guys. He laughed when Kevin told him that I was a madman when it came to taking on work. The two "madmen" were a perfect match working together, as far as Buzz was concerned.

Later in the week, Hector found me an experienced attendant for the weekends named Ramona. He took it upon himself to have her over a couple of days during the week to train her on the finer points of my care. With the weekend care now covered, I was able to feel at ease without any anxiety about how I would manage.

Kandy flew into town during the last week I was working at Buzz's shop and my summer semester was already over, so I was looking forward to spending time with her again, even though we talked almost every day. I left work at lunchtime to pick her up at John Wayne Airport. We met in the lobby, and my heart melted again when I gazed into her emerald-green eyes as I kissed her.

We went back to the shop to finish the day of work, and I introduced her to Kevin and Donny. At the end of the day, Kevin insisted that we take off; he would close up the shop.

As we drove up Pacific Coast Highway to my place, I pointed out spots I liked to hang out in from time to time. We stopped and had dinner before meeting Hector at the small two-bedroom apartment. I made room in the dresser and closet for Kandy to put her things in, and after unpacking, Hector began to get me ready for bed. We were both surprised when Kandy wanted to learn to transfer me to and from the wheelchair—a task that she picked up in about five minutes of going back and forth. As we drifted off to sleep she asked, "So what's the big deal?"

Early the next morning, Hector was there to get me up and ready for work. We showed Kandy my morning bathroom routine and the tiny roll-in shower I used to prepare for the day. When I got back into bed, Kandy learned about the chronic wounds I had to have redressed daily and how I got my clothes on before getting into my chair. She nudged Hector out of the way and transferred me into the chair, straightened my shirt, attached the foot pedals, and combed my hair.

We got into the van to meet Kevin at the shop. The workload was light that day, so we were able to have a picnic lunch in a park down the street. Kevin suggested that he and his girlfriend meet us for dinner that evening at a local sushi bar he knew of. After work, we went to the apartment to get ready for dinner.

Kandy insisted that Hector have the evening off so that we could stay out as long as we wanted to. We arrived at the sushi bar long before the crowd filled the place and got a choice table to enjoy the night. The four of us enjoyed the sushi and had a great conversation getting to know each other. Kevin glanced at his watch at one point and announced that it was time to leave because tomorrow was the last day of work before Buzz returned from his trip.

Kandy and I took our time driving back to Long Beach after dinner. We looked forward to spending as much time as we could with each other without any distractions now that Buzz was coming home.

The next morning, Kandy accompanied me to work as I met Kevin at the gate to open up as usual. Kevin and Donny spent the day working on the scheduled cars and making sure the shop was as clean as it was when Buzz left. I spent the day making appointments with several customers, ordering parts from vendors, and making sure that all the receipts and work orders were organized. Kandy even helped me repair a glitch in the dot matrix printer that Buzz used for his repair orders. At the end of the day, everyone was pleased with the condition of the shop and the front office. Kevin and I were locking the front gate when he leaned over and told me, "That's quite a gal you've got there—I hope you don't do anything to screw it up."

Buzz arrived at the shop on Saturday morning, and I purposely didn't schedule any work, so he'd have the time to go over everything that occurred while he was gone. I introduced him to Kandy as he reviewed the work orders. Eventually, Buzz came out of the office and told me what a great job I had done and that he was very pleased. Kevin, of course, told Buzz that he was ready to kill me at one point because of the amount of work that I'd booked. Buzz laughed and made a few comments about what happens when you put two madmen together.

I brought Kandy with me to the Wednesday afternoon "lunch bunch" group in order to introduce her to all of the guys. After lunch, Dick pulled me aside and whispered into my ear, "John, she's definitely a keeper." Aaron, who was always trying to get a rise out of me, commented that he had no idea what she saw in me. By the time I drove her to LAX so she could fly to her next assignment, it was obvious to both of us that we wanted to pursue a relationship.

When she returned, I greeted her at the gate wearing my John Lennon sunglasses, holding a pencil cup with a cardboard sign draped around my neck that said, "Will work for Kandy." As we embraced, she whispered into my ear what a goofball I was.

The Wednesday Huntington Beach meeting was having an "End of the Summer—Bummer" dance that Saturday night. We went to a nearby café I liked before going to the party. I was so animated with my hands during our conversation that I knocked an entire glass of ice tea onto her lap. She told me that it wasn't a big deal, and as she went to the restroom to dry herself off, I felt like a bumbling high school kid out on his first date. When she returned, we finished our dinners and went to the dance, where I introduced her to even more friends.

At one point during the night, Bob S. pulled me aside and told me that Kandy was a sweetheart, and there was only one person that was going to screw up the relationship—it was the guy looking back at me in the mirror when I shaved in the morning. Bob also shared some wisdom with me that I practice to this day. He told me that in any relationship, romantic or otherwise, I only had two options—to be right or to be happy. That bit of wisdom and insight helped add more clarity to the many of facets of the "life stone" I was constantly working on.

We made the rounds, saying good-bye to everyone as we prepared to leave. When we got in the van, Kandy commented on how many people I knew and that she got the feeling from the crowd she met that night they really were my friends—not just acquaintances, and it touched her...

I started the fall semester excited about the idea of graduating in the spring and finally being done with school. I still had the goal of being an automotive instructor at the college level, armed with my current certificates, licenses, and a degree in automotive technology.

Kandy's next assignment in Grenada was going to last thirty days. I called her every day until I got my phone bill that was a few hundred dollars more than usual. I started to fax her every day instead.

Although we'd been involved for only a few months, I felt as if I'd known her all of my life, especially because of our previous history. I decided to ask her to marry me. A week before the end of her trip, I went to a local jewelry store with my friend Wayne from the Wednesday night Huntington Beach meeting to pick out a ring. He kept asking me if I was jumping the gun and maybe acting a little too rashly, so I decided not to take any chances. I picked out a ring that had diamonds inset in the band, with an emerald marquee in the center. I reasoned that if she said no, I'd still give her the ring as a token of my affection for her, without losing face.

The day before her arrival I made reservations at the Orange County Mining Company, a popular local restaurant on top of a hill that afforded a spectacular view for miles. I'd already asked Kandy if I could take her out to dinner the night she flew in. The entrance to the restaurant was on a narrow, steeply inclined road going up the side of the hill, and the cars were bumper-to-bumper that evening, all the way to the summit.

When we finally made it to the front of the line, the parking lot attendant motioned me to a handicapped spot directly in front of the restaurant. She looked at me in amazement as I said, "I guess it pays to hang out with a gimp."

We talked about her trip while enjoying dinner and the lit-up southern California skyline. We placed our dessert order with the waiter as I told her how much in love with her I was and how I had the feeling we'd known each other for so long... I reached into my vest pocket with one finger to secure the ring I'd placed there earlier. As I pulled out the ring, I asked Kandy if she'd be willing to spend the rest of her life with me and marry me. She had a stunned look on her face and was speechless. I told her, "I'm not asking you to marry me tomorrow—just marry me."

She hugged me, saying yes, and I felt like the luckiest man alive...

Chapter 18
Laughter, Adventures with Hector and Being Grateful

During the next week, I introduced Kandy to even more of my friends and took her to some of the open AA meetings I attended. One of my favorite meetings was the Thursday night Wilson Park group located in Compton. The meeting was held in a ramshackle building that was over fifty years old. Things got exciting that evening as a huge rat ran across the floor, and one of the women attending pulled out a handgun to shoot it. Kandy was at first shocked and alarmed, but her concerns soon dissipated as everyone in the meeting room laughed out loud.

The following night, we attended an awards banquet at the college I went to. I was pleased to introduce her to some of the professors I studied under as well as a few of the staffers at the Disabled Students Center. I received a few awards that evening for my activities as a student body representative and leading the charge in making the radio station handicapped-accessible.

The drive back to the apartment seemed almost anticlimactic because I was thinking ahead about Kandy's next assignment. She was going to spend sixty days in Germany at a military resort installing hardware and software. The thought of not seeing her for two months made me sad because I was going to miss her so much. She later expressed the same sentiment, and we both decided to make the best of it.

Within a couple of days of Kandy's departure, Hector and I packed up the van to attend an AA gathering in Puerto Peñasco, Mexico, commonly referred to as the Rocky Point Convention. I had received an invitation from my friend Nat, who had moved to Arizona a few years earlier. Shortly after crossing the border, I began to feel as if I were on a different planet. Poverty was everywhere in the cities and villages we traveled through. My eyes zeroed in on the smiles on the happy faces of the children every time we made a pit stop, and I realized that they didn't know what they were missing. It made me grateful one more time for the things I had in my life. We crossed a section of barren desert, which, other than the occasional abandoned buildings, seemed to be a wasteland with nothing to see for miles.

We finally arrived at the hotel and needed to check out a few different rooms to find something even remotely accessible for my needs. The room we finally settled on had a drain in the floor of the tiled bathroom so that I could have an improvised shower every day. Hector borrowed a five-gallon bucket from the staff and enjoyed throwing warm water at me from across the room while I sat in the shower chair every morning as we both laughed at the solution we had come up with. The hotel was beautiful and our room had a stunning view of the Sea of Cortez.

With Hector as my interpreter, we explored the city, finding small taco stands where you could buy two soft tacos for fifty cents, and they were absolutely delicious. During one of our forays, we were told about a restaurant on the beach that was touted as the best in town. It was the exact opposite of the hotel we were staying at. Instead of marble flooring, there was sand—instead of upholstered plush furniture, there were plain wooden tables and chairs—instead of ornate glass everywhere, there were screens that allowed the ocean breeze to waft through the small, tin-covered building to cool it because there was no air conditioning. The food was the best I'd ever tasted. Hector and I feasted on seafood, fruit, and vegetables until we were stuffed, receiving a total bill of eleven dollars. It was hilarious to everyone in sight because it took four people to drag me in the wheelchair across the sand back to solid ground when we finally left.

I attended meetings at the conference, reconnecting with Nat and his wife Dianne, as well as other people I hadn't seen for a while. It was a privilege to hear Dr. Paul and his wife Max speak at one of the big meetings (Dr. Paul's story is in the back of the Big Book). Between workshops and meetings, I hung out with friends, puffing on Cuban cigars while people-watching and catching rays, making the year-round suntan I had golden brown. There was no such thing as handicapped parking at any of the places I went to, so I'd park the van diagonally across two spaces in order to lower the ramp without getting blocked in, which again made me grateful for what I had available to me at home. While I did stuff at the convention, Hector did his thing during the day and went clubbing at night.

I called Kandy in Germany one day from the room, and, after twenty minutes, finally got through. The call sounded as if we were talking through two tin cans tied together with string. I told her I was already missing her and that I'd call again when I got home so she'd know everything was okay.

Late one night, I arrived at the hotel room, meeting up with Hector, who had a woman on each arm. I told him about wanting to attend an event the next morning at 6:00 a.m. and asked if he was going to be in good enough shape to get me up. Hector said he would and asked the women to meet him in the bar while he put me in bed.

At 5:00 a.m. he woke me up, asking if he could go to the meeting with me. "Of course," I told him as he got me up for the morning "bucket shower." Hector spied the gazebo next to the pool opening up, and he quickly excused himself. He ran out to the bar and slugged down a Bloody Mary. When he came back, he looked a little better and told me he'd pass on the meeting but thanked me anyway. I made it to the venue a few minutes late and met Hector after he had a few hours of sleep to go to the beach and hang out. The two of us were smoking cigars and enjoying cold drinks (Hector a beer and me an iced tea), tanning, and talking about our adventure so far.

The night before we were to leave, Nat, Dianne, and a few other people insisted that Hector and I join them for dinner at a restaurant at the actual Rocky Point. It was on top of a tall hill on the coast in Puerto Peñasco. We drove up the narrow, winding road to the top of the outcrop and found a parking spot. After we entered the restaurant, five or six people had to lift me onto the raised deck where the eating area was. We sat next to a window facing the water. After about a half an hour, Nat told me to check out the view in the window. We all looked out and saw one of the coolest sights ever. There wasn't a cloud in the sky as the sun was setting. We saw its reflection on the Sea of Cortez and could just make out the Baja Peninsula beyond it. It was well worth the hassle of finding a parking spot and being lifted up and down from the deck to witness that view.

The next morning, we packed up the van, checked out of the hotel, and started the long journey home. Everything was uneventful until we were about halfway through the stretch of desert when I saw two jeeps in the rearview mirror loaded with men wearing military uniforms and holding assault rifles quickly approaching us. One jeep got in front of the van, and they motioned me to pull over. I pulled into an abandoned gas station lot and turned off the van. The soldiers piled out of their jeeps, surrounding us, brandishing their M16s. Hector got out and went to the man who seemed to be in charge. After a few minutes, he came back and said, "Pepe, they think we're carrying drugs or guns, and they want to search the van, so we have to get out."

I lowered the ramp and got out while the men removed everything and searched the luggage. It wasn't until everything was out of the van that they realized it had a lowered floor, making it look as if it were overloaded with contraband. Hector explained to the soldier in charge that the floor was chopped to accommodate my wheelchair so I could drive it. The officer nodded to Hector while motioning his men to load back up in the jeeps, and off they went into the desert, leaving Hector and I (mainly Hector) to repack the van. I was glad that my compadre spoke Spanish and told him so, because I'd have been in the desert or a Mexican jail forever if I was by myself. The rest of the trek went without incident, and the two of us were glad to be home again. I secretly wished I could have kissed the ground because I was back in the United States. After calling Kandy, I went to bed, ready to get back to the grind of school again.

Dick called me within a few days of our return to let me know what was going on with Aaron... His post-polio syndrome had finally caught up to him. He was in a coma at the hospital on life support, and I should get there ASAP.

I arrived at the small waiting room outside of ICU to meet his mother, family members, his girlfriend, and Dick, as well as a few other people close to Aaron. I knew he didn't want to ever be on life support and what the final outcome was going to be. I was still pretty rattled when a doctor came in, telling us it was time for his friends to say their good-byes before the family went into ICU so the staff could remove power from life support and let Aaron go. I spent a moment at his bedside telling him how much he was loved and how he would be missed. I sadly left the room and went outside with my friend, Jerry K. A short time later, I felt a subtle, warm, almost surreal whisper of someone's breath travel up the back of my neck, and I knew my friend was gone...

We got to the ICU as everyone was coming out, and upon seeing me, Aaron's girlfriend draped her arms around my shoulders, giving me a hug. As she sobbed at her loss, she asked me to move over to a nearby area out of earshot of the small crowd. Through her tears, she was able to tell me a few things Aaron never shared with anybody else—how grateful he was for the time I spent with his mother while he was in the ER getting stabilized and that he felt it was a privilege for us to have our kind of friendship. I left the hospital overcome with sadness, but strangely enough, also filled with gratitude...

Chapter 19
Ending a Chapter and Starting Another

I remembered the size of the phone bill I received in early fall of 1996 when Kandy was in Grenada. I used the fax on my computer a lot while she was in Europe. Every night I spent a few minutes going through my dictionary, starting at the beginning, compiled a list of words that began with "A," wrote a love note using those specific words, and faxed it to her the next morning. Over time, I went through every letter of the alphabet, composing love notes using the letter of the day. Kandy told me later that the staff at the hotel were as excited about her daily faxes as she was.

After spending the holidays with her family in Cleveland, Kandy flew into town just in time for the New Year's Eve party that had become a tradition. I've got to admit I was a little jealous of Frank H. as he and Kandy did some ballroom dancing across the floor before the party began. As dinner started, I was happy to see that the place was packed. We enjoyed a great meal, followed by a speaker meeting. Dr. Paul and his wife, Max, gave enjoyable talks regarding their mutual story from their own perspectives. The festivities went on late into the night. The stroke of midnight came and went as Kandy and I kissed and wished each other, as well as our friends, a happy new year.

On the way home, we talked about exciting prospects for 1997. I was graduating from college in the early summer and would hopefully find a job teaching someplace. We even talked about the possibility of moving in together.

Over the next few days, I told Kandy about the strange things that happened to me outside of the hospital when Aaron passed away, his funeral, and the fact that I missed him, even though at times he was such a pain in the butt. When the subject of spring break came up, Kandy suggested that I think about driving to Cleveland for a few days and seeing her family, since I hadn't seen them in twenty years. I thought about it, and as the idea became more appealing, we decided on a plan.

In late March, after completing an assignment she arrived in Los Angeles to accompany me on the road trip as my navigator. We spent one night in a hotel, but other than that, I drove straight through so we could spend more time visiting with her family.

We arrived at her ground-floor apartment in a suburb just west of Cleveland and were pleased to see that the complex manager took the time to designate a handicapped parking spot and make a little ramp for me to get on the sidewalk so I could enter her building.

After sleeping about twelve hours, we had coffee with a small breakfast and got ready for the day. The size and floor plan of Kandy's apartment made it relatively easy to get me into the shower chair and conduct the usual morning routine. She finished getting herself ready, and we went to the van to drive to her sister Kim's house in a neighboring town about six miles away.

Once I was inside and everything settled down, I got reacquainted with her immediate family, as well as their spouses and their children. I recognized Kandy's mother and her sister, Kim, right away, and as time went on, I picked up on the resemblance to the vague images I had in my mind of her other siblings because they were so young the last time I saw them. It seemed to break the ice a little when the subject of recovery came up because her youngest brother, Carl, and his fiancé, Dawn, were in the program.

Carl, who was three or four years sober at the time, irritated me as he started what seemed to be an interrogation. I remember thinking to myself, *This guy was a nine or ten-year-old rug rat the last time I saw him, and who does he think he is?* I had to bite my tongue, however, because I had a rap sheet, so I answered all of his questions to the best of my ability.

We had a great visit over the next couple of days, even taking some of Kandy's nieces and nephews to the Natural History Museum downtown. I was able to kill two birds with one stone, since while entertaining and getting to know the kids, I also collected information for a term paper soon due in an archaeology class I was taking at school. I said my good-byes to Kandy's family, and as we started driving back to southern California, the coolest thing happened... It was late March, and the Hale-Bopp comet was plainly visible to the naked eye in the night sky. It appeared in front of the van with its long white tail every night, as if it were guiding me home.

As graduation approached, it was becoming obvious that my dream of becoming a shop teacher wasn't going to happen. I shared my frustration and disappointment with Kandy, and she suggested that, since we planned to live together anyway, I should consider moving to Cleveland, possibly finding better prospects there. After some thought, I agreed to try it for a year because I'd never been through a snowy winter in my wheelchair and didn't know whether I could handle it. I also stressed the importance of finding a place that was handicapped-accessible and also included a roll-in shower. I honestly thought it was going to be difficult to find a place that met those requirements.

Kandy and Kim found a single-story condo for sale within two weeks, just down the street from Kim's house. I called the woman who was selling the condo and negotiated a one-year lease with an option to buy it, just in case. We decided to be in Cleveland on July 1 because Arik, one of the guys I sponsored, had asked me to be the best man at his wedding.

I graduated from college at the end of May, overcome with emotion as I sat with my fellow students waiting to receive our diplomas. I was thinking to myself that this was the first time in my life I had actually followed through and finished something. I was graduating with honors, adding icing to the cake. I looked up into the stands and saw Kandy, Hector, Dick, his wife Loretta, as well as a lot of other close friends there to support me. After the ceremony, we all got together to have lunch and celebrate the occasion. Even my buddy Bob Gillespie, an alumnus of the college, was there.

A few weeks later, Kandy and I went to see a friend on a Saturday night, and I was shocked to find out that she'd secretly put together a surprise going-away party for me. At any given time during the evening, there had to be at least a hundred people milling about. A few months later, Wayne mailed me a scrapbook full of pictures and written comments from a lot of the folks there that night. There is one picture in the scrapbook that is special to me—it's a photo of our immediate "sobriety family," reflecting eight generations of sponsorship! So once again the Big Book is right when it talks about seeing a fellowship grow up about you.

On the night of Arik's wedding, we said our good-byes to friends because we were leaving the next day. Hector came early the next morning to shower me, dress me, and get me up and ready for the trip. As he helped us load the van, I tearfully said good-bye to the buddy I'd gotten so tight with over the years. Kandy and I hit the road to start our new adventure...

Just like the first visit to Ohio, other than spending a night in a hotel just to get some sleep, I drove straight through, and we met the movers right on time. A few of Kandy's family members were there to help us, and the movers put all the big stuff where we wanted it in the condo. As everything was getting put into place, I had the feeling deep inside that this was exactly where I was supposed to be. We, of course, purchased the condo when the lease was up.

During the next few months, Kandy was on the road so much that I had a lot of time to go to meetings all over the place. I found a new sponsor, Tom M., within two weeks and started making new friends at many of the local meetings I went to.

I was telling Kandy's brother Carl one night that I was having trouble finding newcomers to work with. He said that the best place to find them was at halfway houses and suggested that I check out a place in Cleveland called the Freedom House. I was talking to Tom one night about Carl's suggestion when he told me that he did a Big Book study there with his sponsor Don and invited me to join them. I took him up on his offer and soon started working with, as well as sponsoring, some of the guys in the house.

Kandy grew tired of traveling so much and started searching for a local job. Shortly thereafter, she accepted a job at the Sheraton Cleveland Airport Hotel. Her new position would allow us to spend more time together.

I became a fixture at the Freedom House, and they soon offered me a job as a counselor. Because of my social security income, I was only allowed to earn a maximum of $500 a month, so it was no big strain on their budget. I remembered Polly suggesting that I become a counselor when I was in treatment, and I'd been resistant to the idea at the time—look at what I was doing now...

Note: I started taking a few of the guys with me regularly on Thursday afternoons to Rosary Hall, the oldest treatment center in the United States, started by Sister Ignatius in 1950, in downtown Cleveland. We began a Big Book study with patients in the detox ward. When a person is detoxing from whatever he or she has been doing, they normally don't have the ability to retain much, so the study was confined to "The Doctor's Opinion." I did this for a couple of reasons—to show the guys I brought with me that they did have something offer and hopefully see a patient's "light bulb" come on as I explained the chapter, paragraph by paragraph, like the old-timers did for me when I was new...

A few months later, I was asked to consider writing grant proposals for the house in order to help raise operating funds. I had no idea what was involved in the process but agreed to give it a try. After doing some research, I approached the St. Luke's Foundation and was fortunate to find a kind program officer who showed me the ropes of grant-writing. The house was awarded its first grant because of her help, and I began a new segment of my career. I began filling out applications and writing proposals on a regular basis and started to develop a measure of success in my efforts, even while continuing to work with the guys.

Note: I love working with new guys, especially when they're having trouble with the steps. One of the things I used to do when I found out that a man was having difficulty completing his fourth step was to ask him to meet me in my office with his Big Book and a pen at a certain time.

I made sheets on my computer with columns already on them for the resentment list as well as the fear list. When they came in and sat down, I gave them a few sheets of paper already labeled for the resentment list.

I would ask them to list the people, places, and institutions with whom they were pissed off in the far left column, labeled "I'm resentful at," and go down the entire column until they were done.

I would then ask them to go back to the top of the first page and start down the second column labeled "the cause" and fill in the blocks all the way down until they were done. This was repeated with the third column, labeled "what it affects."

When the third column was complete, we would go back to the beginning, and I'd quiz them as they went through the fourth column, labeled "my part in it," until everything was filled in. We did the same process for the fears list.

I would then have them grab a blank sheet of paper and write a list of names of people they had relationships with. They would then turn their Big Books to page 69, and I'd ask them to write down their answers to the six questions related to sex conduct in regard to each of the relationships they had listed.

When we were finished, I would talk to them about the deep, dark secrets, stressing how important it was that they come clean with everything, or they would pay the price, saying that anything they told me would never leave the office. When they came clean and fessed up everything, I'd ask them for a hug and tell them what a great job they just did.

When I asked a man what he just did, often I got a blank look. I'd tell them "Dude, not only did you just finish your fourth step, but you did your fifth as well!" The astonished looks on their faces were priceless as I suggested that it was now time for them to move on with the rest of the steps...

I started another Tuesday night CBS group in our living room using the format that we had with the original group in California, and it became a Big Book "step study." Within a few months, there were so many people packed in our small living room for the meeting on Tuesday nights that it had to be moved to a Methodist church in neighboring Avon Lake—it's listed in the area directory and still meets to this day.

Kandy and I set our wedding date for September 10, 1999, and I knew I needed to make amends to her mother before we were married. It was one of the toughest ones I've ever done. We agreed to meet in a park close to her house on the east side of Cleveland. I showed up, and after some small talk, I got down to business admitting my faults and the many wrongs I committed that affected her and the family while Kandy and I were together in the 1970s. I copped to everything I could remember and asked her the first question—I sat there listening as she recounted many other things I'd done, and tears began to stream down my face—because I didn't have a leg to stand on. I remembered everything as she told me and didn't say a word. When I asked the second question, she said, "I think Kandy is out of her mind for wanting to marry you, but she's a grown woman and can do whatever she pleases. Don't you ever hurt my daughter." Today she tells me on a regular basis that she loves me. I refer to her as "Mom," and she lovingly calls me "Grasshopper."

Our wedding was one to remember because of all the love that filled the room. For the second time in my life, I experienced a look of unconditional love coming from another human being, while my bride and I gazed at each other as she walked down the aisle. Hector had recently moved to Ohio to work for me and was my best man. Some of the guys that I sponsored in California were in the wedding party, as well as my sponsor, Tom, and a few other close friends that I'd met in the meetings. Kandy's sister Kim was the maid of honor. Her other sister Dawn, her niece Caitlyn, and her close friends from Florida were in the wedding party as well. I was honored that Dick and his wife Loretta flew from California to be there and share this momentous occasion with us.

All of the people attending our reception remarked about what an amazing evening it was. The next morning, we went to Key West for our honeymoon and had the time of our lives.

Chapter 20
Giving Back

One afternoon I was at work getting ready to do a group session with the guys when I got a phone call from my sister Linda letting me know that my mother had just passed away. I knew she was on her deathbed but couldn't be there because I was on the waiting list at the Cleveland Clinic for kidney surgery to remove a cancerous mass that had been discovered. I was so shaken up that I was in no shape emotionally to conduct the group and had to go home.

For the first time in years, the thought of having a drink was more than that... I knew exactly what I had to do. After spending some time talking to Kandy, I went to a meeting and found somebody relatively new to talk to so that I was able to get out myself for a while and didn't have to drink. It works—it really does!

I learned that when you've got cancer in your kidneys, it can't be treated with chemotherapy or radiation; the mass has to be surgically removed. After I was finally able to be admitted to the Cleveland Clinic, one third of my lower right kidney was cut out in hopes that they got it all. While I was recuperating in my hospital room, the surgeon came in and told me that during the course of the operation they unexpectedly discovered that the lower third of my left kidney was missing as well—it was probably removed following my car accident while at the Trauma Center because of the extent of the internal damage. After a regime of CAT scans every six months, I was pronounced cancer-free a few years later.

In the early spring of 2000, Kandy and I'd just ordered a new minivan. It was completed just in time for me to give it its break-in drive to Minneapolis for my first world convention. It was awesome to hear well over forty thousand people recite the Lord's prayer in the stadium at the end of the gathering. Other than the pounding rainstorms, the drive home was uneventful, and I was happy with the way everything worked on the van.

Over the next few years, I continued working for Freedom House, attending meetings, doing 12-Step work, and sponsoring my monkeys.

Note: I've always referred to the guys I sponsor as "monkeys," because they're constantly getting into stuff. I also make it a point of telling them that they've done more for my sobriety than they'll ever know... Often, I'll receive looks telling me they didn't understand—and that's when I lay down the gauntlet, "daring" them to take the steps, apply what they learn in their lives, and help someone. I can't tell you how many "monkeys" have come to me later, letting me know they finally understood what I was talking about when they were new...

In early 2003, I came up with the idea of partnering with several treatment centers in the Cleveland area and putting on a two-night comedy show in an effort to create public awareness, starring a nationally known comedian I knew, Mark L., who's in recovery himself. Each of the treatment centers was going to chip in a dollar amount to cover the expenses for the event. After receiving an anonymous donation to cover part of the cost, I arranged to partner with Lorain County Alcohol and Drug Abuse Services (LCADA) and Rosary Hall and did the show at Cuyahoga Community College that summer. We ended up losing money because of the small turnout, and Mark was kind enough to adjust his price, so the financial hit we took wasn't so bad. An idea began to form in the back of my mind, however, as a result of this experience that would come to fruition down the road.

It was late summer that year when Freedom House and I parted ways. Not having a job during the day freed me up to do even more 12-Step work. I volunteered to become a member of the Alcohol and Drug Addiction Services (ADAS) Board of Lorain County and was with them for the next year. I was also bringing an extra meeting in to a local prison every Friday and conducting a group on Wednesday mornings with the guys at the Lantern, a halfway house in Cleveland, before going to a noon Big Book study I chaired at the Saharid Club not far away.

A few of us started the meeting at the club because the time slot was open and there wasn't a Big Book study anywhere on their schedule. We named it the "Rule 62 Big Book Group" and had it listed in the local area meeting directory. Rule 62 is "don't take yourself so damned seriously," and its origins are discussed in the twelve-and-twelve.

There were only a dozen people or so attending the first meeting, but within a few months the place was packed. It wasn't uncommon to have sixty or seventy people in attendance. Once we had over a hundred people jammed into the room for a lunchtime meeting! Every year, when the time came to elect new officers, the "railroad committee" would come out of the woodwork and elect me as their chair for one more term. We started a tradition that, when the treasury allowed it, we'd buy a case of Big Books at a time so everyone attending the meeting would have a book in front of them, and we always made a point of giving a book to any new person who didn't own one. During the course of nine years we gave away well over a thousand Big Books!

During this time, I started my own small nonprofit, calling it Rule 62 Fundraising, receiving several donations to get it off the ground. LCADA split the expenses with me for the 2004 summer comedy show, and we broke even. I decided from that point on to have a one-night-only show, and it became a yearly event, with the sole purpose of raising money to help indigent people get into treatment. What began as a kernel of an idea grew to become a week-long event as Rule 62 Fundraising became self-sufficient. Mark and I would spend the week going to area jails, prisons, and treatment centers, putting on free shows. That year I added a recovery golf benefit to the agenda the day before the big show on Saturday night—both were open to the public.

I was able to recruit volunteers from both in and out of the meetings, forming a "core" group to help put on the events. But the most valuable volunteer was Kandy because she is so organized and was able to deal with things that popped up while Mark and I were on the road. During the golf outings, she was in charge of the money and showed the crew of volunteers how to streamline the registration process for the golfers so they'd get out onto the course and play, while I'd mingle with the participants. At the Saturday night comedy show, Kandy would be in the lobby taking ticket money and helping the crew with anything they needed, while I'd be in the auditorium making sure the show went smoothly for whatever opening act we had that year and for Mark. The experience became our passion, and we've always made sure that down payments were made almost immediately after the week was over in preparation for the following year. Over the years, Rule 62 Fundraising has been able to donate thousands of dollars to area treatment centers as a way to give back.

In the fall of 2004, I was hired by LCADA as a grant writer. I resigned from the ADAS Board so that it wouldn't be a conflict of interest. I found myself in uncharted territory because most of the foundations I dealt with while working at Freedom House looked at Lorain County, a rural community, as a third-world country. So I started looking at federal grants as a means of supporting the agency. After a lot of research and learning "federaleese" (the lingo spoken at the federal level), I started applying for grants, and we've managed to raise several million dollars for the organization over the ensuing years. At one point, I was asked to help the mayor's office in the city of Lorain apply for a three-year twelve million dollar project. The federal grant was awarded to the city, but was only funded for two years. These efforts have filled me with an overwhelming sense of gratification, since it is another way of giving back.

In the late fall of 2006, a meeting was started at my house on Saturdays for our immediate "sobriety family." Some of the monkeys would show up early or stay late to help me with the motorcycle trike project I had going on in my garage. I was building a trike from the ground up that I could drive from my wheelchair, and the guys were invaluable in helping me. My sponsor, Tom, showed up one Saturday for the meeting, and I have a photograph that I cherish showing six generations of sponsorship.

In 2009, I received a call from the Northern Ohio Recovery Association, inviting me to its annual dinner to receive the award as Lorain County's Recovery Advocate of the year. I've always tried to do everything I do under the radar and immediately felt uncomfortable with the idea. After talking to Dick in California and my sponsor Tom, both gave me the same advice. They told me to go to the banquet, eat my "rubber chicken," and accept the award. Kandy and I drove downtown to the venue. When they announced my name to receive the award, I rolled up the ramp onto the stage and was handed the microphone say a few words. I told the audience that I was uncomfortable and dedicated the award to "all those people that didn't know that they didn't know."

Kandy and I were the only two people in the elevator as the doors closed when we were leaving that night. A hand popped out of nowhere to open the doors, and there was a young blond woman standing before us. The woman looked at us and then directly at me and said, "John, you don't remember me, but six years ago I was in detox at Rosary Hall, and you took the time to talk to me—I've been sober ever since, and I just wanted to thank you." The doors closed on the elevator, and as we went down to the parking structure, a single tear rolled down my cheek because that experience alone was worth a hundred "rubber chicken" dinners...

In 2010, my brother Bob passed away from cancer that he kept secret from everyone except my sister Betty. Kandy and I flew to northern Maine for his funeral, where I was able to give a short impromptu eulogy for the man who saved my life so many years ago. Betty was able to see Kandy and I interact with each other during the few days we were there, remarking about what a lucky man I was to have her in my life. Betty and I sorted out some of the misunderstandings that occurred over the years, and we've been tight ever since.

In early 2012, Kandy received a job offer in Daytona Beach, Florida. We both decided that it sounded like a great opportunity, so in April she went to Daytona Beach, staying at the hotel while we were having a new house built. My assignment was to get our current home in Ohio ready to sell and to finish the trike I was still building in the garage.

Kandy was able to come back to town and help out with the Rule 62 Fundraising events because it was becoming so big and successful. The golf outing had been selling out for the last few years, and attendance at the Saturday night show was on the increase. I changed the name of the nonprofit to Rule 62 Productions and turned over control of the company to Jim S., one of the original board members, who was now the vice president. It turned out to be a banner year, and we were able to make donations to six different halfway houses.

My wife surprised me when she snuck into town for our wedding anniversary. We talked and decided that our original plan was going to take too long because we missed each other so much. I talked to a friend who owned a moving company, making arrangements to pack up the entire house, move everything, and meet them in Daytona Beach on November 1, when escrow closed on our new home.

During the last few weeks of October, there were many tearful good-byes to the many friends who had become so near and dear to me. Larry V., an old-timer at one of the meetings I attended, gave me John W.'s phone number in Daytona Beach to contact once I got there. Larry was his sponsor and told me John had moved to the area a few years earlier, was pretty active in the recovery community, and would be a great way to "plug in" and get involved. Larry knew of my wish to start Rule 62 Fundraising in Florida and thought John could help me network with the people I needed to, so that I'd be able to start a new tradition in the area.

I left North Ridgeville with Kandy's best friend Patty B. riding shotgun as my navigator, ready to begin another new adventure...It took nineteen hours (I napped for three hours) for Patty and I to get to Daytona Beach. Kandy was there when we arrived, and after I checked out our new place, the moving van pulled up. Everything went like clockwork as we unloaded the van and placed everything throughout the house. Patty was able to spend a few days with us, helping Kandy get the house in order.

I contacted John and started going to meetings. I met him at a noon meeting held at the Almous Club, only six or seven miles away from our house. I immediately adopted the "Way of Life Group" that meets six days a week there as my new home group. The first day I went there to meet John happened to be my twenty-sixth sober anniversary, so the group asked me to give a talk that afternoon, and it served as a way of breaking the ice to let people know a little about me.

Within two or three months of moving to Daytona Beach, I started to have health problems related to the chronic pressure ulcers I'd been dealing with for years. My new medical insurance plan allowed me have access to a doctor that was the first in Florida to be certified as a wound care specialist. For the next couple of years I saw the doctor regularly, as well as other specialists, to treat my deteriorating condition.

In early 2014, we discovered, quite by accident, that I've had a bone infection for years. It's so extensive that it covers my entire left leg and the left side of my pelvis. That same year we also found out that I've had a deep-tissue infection as well. Throughout the year, I was taken to the hospital on eight different occasions, and the doctors have come to the conclusion that the infections I've been carrying all this time are intertwined and incurable.

That fall, my youngest sister, Linda, died from cancer. Even though she knew why I couldn't physically be there, I still felt guilty. We talked long and often on the phone as she went through the regime of chemotherapy and radiation treatments that proved to be fruitless in the end...

After spending the entire month of February 2015 and the latter part of March in the hospital, I was told that I probably have three to six months to live...

In all honesty, I've got to tell you that after the news sank in, I was angry with God, because I moved to Florida with the purest of intentions—to help someone by continuing to do the things I've done for years. After a couple of weeks of listening to the "silly nonsense" going on between my ears, my thinking began to change for the good. I began to get in touch with my "attitude of gratitude" again, for, after all, I've been given twenty-eight extra years I didn't deserve (according to the negativity that my mind still sometimes suffers from), and I've gotten to spend the last nineteen years with the love of my life. How many people can say that?

Although three to six months are only numbers, I know that God's really in charge, and I'll go in His and in His time only. My situation has dictated, however, that I deal with some of the realities I'm facing. I started with a local hospice care agency over two months ago, which has been a tremendous relief for both Kandy and I. Even though my medical insurance has provided home health care for me, Kandy, my extraordinary wife, has been my primary caretaker since I moved here, because we haven't found a person with the necessary aptitude and skills to be my personal care assistant.

The outpouring of love from the guys I've sponsored in Cleveland and from her family has been phenomenal, because many of them have made the trip here to spend time with us as I enter this final chapter of my life. I haven't been able to drive for a year and a half because it wasn't safe, so I've missed going to meetings when and where I wished. A few months ago, I sold the van that had been sitting in the garage all this time for a few hundred dollars, because it was fifteen years old, and I've certainly gotten my money's worth out of it. I'm still working for the treatment center in Ohio, and Kandy is now working part-time in order to keep her medical insurance. I've written my Last Will and Testament, and the Power of Attorney document is complete, as well as the rest of my personal loose ends.

I started my journey of recovery with a "life stone" that was flawed and misshapen so badly that it was unrecognizable to anyone, especially me, who looked at it. Through the years of effort at taking the steps and making them a central part of my life, I've managed to chip away at the rough edges and polish its many facets to produce a stone that's totally unique.

I still have many flaws, but what's different today about my "life stone" is that everything in it is crystal clear—I can see everything for what it really is because I'm no longer carrying any extra baggage, and I don't have any secrets to hide. I believe that I'm now the man our beagle Jasper always thought I was before he passed away in 2011. I've finally learned the answer to the question I always asked: "What's in it for me?" *I'm free.*

Words somehow fall short in trying to express how truly grateful I am for the many mentors I've had, the monkeys I've been privileged to work with, and my friends and family—especially Kandy, who has been an example for me about how to give and receive unconditional love, no matter what. But most importantly, I'm grateful for the God I've discovered on my journey, who has helped me become the man I am today over the course of the last 10,521 days but who's counting?

Made in the USA
Middletown, DE
27 September 2016